▶ Military Internees, Prisoners of War and the
Irish State during the Second World War

DOI: 10.1057/9781137446039.0001

Other Palgrave Pivot titles

Michael Byron: Submission and Subjection in Leviathan: Good Subjects in the Hobbesian Commonwealth

Andrew Szanajda: The Allies and the German Problem, 1941–1949: From Cooperation to Alternative Settlement

Joseph E. Stiglitz and Refet S. Gürkaynak: Taming Capital Flows: Capital Account Management in an Era of Globalization

Amelia Lambelet and Raphael Berthele: Age and Foreign Language Learning in School

Justin Robertson: Localizing Global Finance: The Rise of Western-Style Private Equity in China

Isabel Dulfano: Indigenous Feminist Narratives: I/We: Wo(men) of an(Other) Way

Stefan Lund: School Choice, Ethnic Divisions, and Symbolic Boundaries

Daniel Wirls: The Federalist Papers and Institutional Power: In American Political Development

Marcus Morgan and Patrick Baert: Conflict in the Academy: A Study in the Sociology of Intellectuals

Robyn Henderson and Karen Noble: Professional Learning, Induction and Critical Reflection: Building Workforce Capacity in Education

Graeme Kirkpatrick: The Formation of Gaming Culture: UK Gaming Magazines, 1981–1995

Candice C. Carter: Social Education for Peace: Foundations, Teaching, and Curriculum for Visionary Learning

Dilip K. Das: An Enquiry into the Asian Growth Model

Jan Pakulski and Bruce Tranter: The Decline of Political Leadership in Australia? Changing Recruitment and Careers of Federal Politicians

Christopher W. Hughes: Japan's Foreign and Security Policy under the 'Abe Doctrine': New Dynamism or New Dead End?

palgrave▸pivot

Military Internees, Prisoners of War and the Irish State during the Second World War

Bernard Kelly
University of Edinburgh, UK

palgrave
macmillan

DOI: 10.1057/9781137446039.0001

First published 2015 by
PALGRAVE MACMILLAN

Palgrave Macmillan in the UK is an imprint of Macmillan Publishers Limited, registered in England, company number 785998, of Houndmills, Basingstoke, Hampshire RG21 6XS.

Palgrave Macmillan in the US is a division of St Martin's Press LLC, 175 Fifth Avenue, New York, NY 10010.

Palgrave Macmillan is the global academic imprint of the above companies and has companies and representatives throughout the world.

Palgrave® and Macmillan® are registered trademarks in the United States, the United Kingdom, Europe and other countries.

ISBN: 978-1-137-44602-2 EPUB
ISBN: 978-1-137-44603-9 PDF
ISBN: 978-1-137-44601-5 Hardback

A catalogue record for this book is available from the British Library.

A catalog record for this book is available from the Library of Congress.

www.palgrave.com/pivot

DOI: 10.1057/9781137446039

Contents

DOI: 10.1057/9781137446039.0001

Acknowledgements

A number of people have helped enormously in the writing of this book. Dwight Meares at the US Military Academy at West Point and John Reynolds of the Garda College deserve special mention for kindly sending on both documents and the results of their research. Thanks also to Michael Kennedy of the Royal Irish Academy for his assistance in deciphering Department of Foreign Affairs files. I wish to acknowledge the assistance of the Director and staff of the National Archives of Ireland, the Irish Military Archives, the University College Dublin Archives, the Columban Archives and the National Library. I am indebted to Tomás Kenny for his constant supply of books and his perceptive insights on Irish history. Finally, none of my work would ever be possible without the patience, forbearance and support of my wife Monica and daughter Sophia, to whom I owe everything.

DOI: 10.1057/9781137446039.0002

Introduction

Kelly, Bernard. *Military Internees, Prisoners of War and the Irish State during the Second World War.* Basingstoke: Palgrave Macmillan, 2015.
DOI: 10.1057/9781137446039.0003.

▶

During the Second World War, neutral Ireland (then also known as Eire) interacted with military internees and prisoners of war both inside and outside the island of Ireland: members of the belligerent forces incarcerated in Eire, prisoners of war (including Irish) held abroad in Europe and Asia, and German prisoners of war detained in Northern Ireland, which was still a part of the United Kingdom. As a neutral, Eire was required by international law to arrest and intern members of the belligerent forces who made landfall in the 26 counties and as a result, between 1940 and 1945 a total of 45 Allied aircrew and 269 Axis airmen and sailors were held at the Curragh military camp. The Allied personnel consisted of 31 British, eight Canadians, three Poles, one Frenchman, one New Zealander and an American, described on the official internee list as 'Yanks (USA)'.[1] The lone American was a member of the RAF; no US military personnel were ever interned. Situated in county Kildare, around 30 miles from Dublin, the Curragh camp was (and remains) the largest military complex in Ireland. First constructed in 1855, it served as a military base and police depot until it passed into the hands of the Dublin government after the foundation of the Irish Free State in 1922. The belligerent internees in the Curragh were initially classed as prisoners of war, in order for the government to extend the 1907 Hague and 1929 Geneva Conventions to them, and also to establish a basis for their treatment: what food, clothes and medical treatment they were entitled to, where and how they were to be detained, whether they had to work or not and what privileges the government could offer them. Apart from a brief period between August and October 1940, they were not actually *treated* as prisoners of war and were granted an extensive range of concessions, such as permission to leave the camp on parole. From 1942 onwards, when Dublin altered the legislative basis of its belligerent interment regime, they were categorised as 'military internees' and all references to them as 'prisoners of war' were dropped.

There were, in fact, two internment camps at the Curragh during the war. No.1 internment camp, known amongst its inmates as 'Tintown', was reserved for IRA members and other republican detainees, interned under emergency law for the duration of the war. The second, No.2 internment camp – also known as 'K-Lines' – was where the belligerent personnel were held. K-Lines was divided into two sections: 'B' camp for Allied prisoners and 'G' camp for the Axis.[2] The identifiers 'B' and 'G' were originally applied when there were just British and German

DOI: 10.1057/9781137446039.0003

personnel interned, but they remained even after different nationalities began to enter the Allied compound.

A further issue for the de Valera government to grapple with were the thousands of German prisoners of war who were held in camps in Northern Ireland during 1944–45, and whose presence had the potential to cause serious difficulties for Dublin. As part of the UK, Northern Ireland took part in the conflict, but because of the complicated political and security situation there, prisoners of war were not held in Ulster until late in the war when the British government had no choice owing of the lack of accommodation in Britain. When considering the internee/prisoner of war issue, the Dublin government devoted the bulk of its time to K-Lines and the belligerent internees held there; as a neutral, it could do little to intervene on behalf of Irish prisoners of war abroad, and Germans arrived in Northern Ireland only at the very end of the war. This book reflects this reality. While it explores the attitude of the de Valera government towards prisoners of war both on the island of Ireland and outside, it concentrates mainly on the belligerent internment policy and the military internees within K-Lines and subsequent camps.

Running through the internment and prisoner of war issues like a thread was the emphasis placed by Dublin on their international importance. The fact that Ireland was detaining members of the armed forces of the warring powers carried obvious diplomatic consequences. Representatives of the belligerents were frequent visitors to the camp, and the detainees had regular and unsupervised access to their consular officials. Any allegations of mistreatment or dissatisfaction with life in the camp could quickly escalate into an international incident. Accordingly, the de Valera government took great care to ensure that K-Lines (and other subsequent belligerent camps) did not become a point of contention between Ireland and the warring powers. The wide range of liberties given to the internees, both Allied and German, was partly driven by the need to avoid friction with the belligerent nations. Although the Department of Defence and the Irish military had primary responsibility for guarding the camp, it was the Department of External Affairs which had the final say on issues such as parole, living conditions and punishments. De Valera – who was both Taoiseach and Minister for External Affairs throughout the war – and top-rank officials within External Affairs such as secretary Joseph Walshe, assistant secretary Frederick Boland and legal advisor Michael Rynne were all closely involved in the running of K-Lines, as were the German and Allied ministers in Dublin.

DOI: 10.1057/9781137446039.0003

Furthermore, Ireland's relationship with the Allies, in particular the United States, altered the belligerent internment regime as the war went on. After America entered the conflict, the Irish government made a decision not to intern US aircrew under any circumstances, and used the convenient fiction of distinguishing between 'operational' and 'non-operational' flights to achieve this. All American personnel who made landfall in Ireland were freed, regardless of the circumstance of their arrival. This imbalance soon led to pressure from London for the same consideration, which eventually led to the release of all Allied internees in two batches, the first in October 1943 and the second in June 1944. From 1942 onwards, despite a handful of RAF personnel still being detained after landing, Dublin operated its belligerent internment regime almost entirely in favour of the Allies. Berlin was unable to prevent this as its military and diplomatic position eroded rapidly from 1943. Seen from this point of view, internment of belligerent personnel was embedded within neutrality and was altered accordingly as Ireland leaned heavily towards the Allies as the war went on.

The Second World War was not the first time foreign military person-nel were imprisoned in Ireland. In 1915, during the First World War, 2,300 German prisoners of war were held in Richmond Barracks in Tipperary, in what is now the training college of the Garda Síochaná (Irish police force).[3] This predated Irish independence and the Irish Free State did not come into existence until December 1922. Ironically, some of these men ended up interacting with an Irish member of the RAF who was shot down in March 1945 and captured by the Germans.[4] With no previous experience of imprisoning foreign military personnel, during the Second World War the Irish government initially relied on international conventions regarding prisoners of war. However, Dublin's policy evolved as the war went on and by 1942 the de Valera government was confident enough to move away from international prisoner of war regulations and establish a new legislative foundation for interning belligerents, based on Irish emergency law. Again, diplomatic consid-erations were consistently prioritised over the strict implementation of international law in the Irish attitude towards belligerent internees and the internment system as a whole. In this, Ireland was not alone and all European neutrals tailored their belligerent internment regimes to suit their own particular situations. In reality, only Switzerland adhered to international law; instead the rest, like Ireland, ignored it when it was to their advantage.

DOI: 10.1057/9781137446039.0003

Prisoners of war, whether they were Irish citizens in the British forces or Germans in Northern Ireland, also posed a series of problems for the de Valera government during the war. Dublin's ability to intercede on behalf of Irish prisoners of war was extremely limited. Indeed, it was a topic that Dublin was sometimes keen to avoid. In any case, Dublin had no legal authority to intervene on behalf of Irish citizens in military captivity and a very small diplomatic network to operate through. The government only really became concerned when there were potential diplomatic concerns, such as German attempts to recruit Irish prisoners for anti-British activities. There were also routine issues such as Irish families sending letters and packages from Ireland to their relatives in captivity and the very sensitive question of German prisoners of war escaping from Northern Ireland and the continent to seek refuge in the 26 counties. When dealing with the latter, which had the potential to severely damage the Irish-British relationship, Dublin shelved international neutral practice entirely and created its own policy, which was veiled in secrecy and shielded from both the press and the Irish parliament.

One of the greatest misconceptions regarding K-Lines was that it was a prisoner-of-war camp. It was not and was never intended to be one. Dublin's motivations for arresting and detaining belligerent personnel were completely different from the warring powers' rationale for capturing enemy personnel. It was not remotely in de Valera's, or Ireland's, interest to treat the military internees as prisoners of war. The concessions the internees enjoyed during the war were mirrored across neutrals in Europe, particularly in Sweden and Switzerland, both of which held many more belligerent personnel than Ireland. Stephen Tanner has observed that US aircrew joked about the easy life of Allied internees in Switzerland, but many who ended up in Swiss custody were disappointed to find that food was rationed and lacking in material comforts.[5] Indeed, Richard Overy has suggested that a slump in USAF morale contributed to 89 bomber crews choosing to land in either Sweden or Switzerland during March and April 1944 alone,[6] as Allied losses were running at high levels and German resistance refused to crack. Dublin deliberately attempted to model its military internment regime on the Swedish and Swiss examples, and there are repeated references in Irish government documents to how both these countries treated their belligerent internees. De Valera's decision to release Allied personnel as the war neared its end was also in step with other neutrals. Sweden, Turkey, Spain and

DOI: 10.1057/9781137446039.0003

Portugal all set Allied internees free as German defeat became more and more obvious. The extant literature on the belligerent internees in Ireland almost entirely overlooks this, instead treating K-Lines as if it was some sort of anomaly or as a typically Irish solution to the internment problem. The aim of this work is to place the belligerent internment regime in Ireland into its proper context, alongside other European neutrals, and to steer it away from comparisons with prisoners of war, which are pointless and do not offer us any real insights. Its dual argument is that diplomatic considerations were uppermost in de Valera's mind when implementing belligerent internment policy, and that the life of the men in K-Lines was not unlike those detained in belligerent internment camps across neutral Europe.

Misconceptions abound in the literature concerning military internment in Ireland during the Second World War. T. Ryle Dwyer's *Guests of the State* described K-Lines as a species of concentration camp[7] and reads more like a novel than a work of history. However, one of its most useful aspects is that the author carried out interviews with many of the men in the camp, and the Irish army officers guarding them, although this is somewhat overshadowed by the author's insistence on recreating spoken dialogue between the men and the lack of references in the text. Despite these frustrating flaws, it remains a worthwhile work, particularly when combined with his broader book on Irish-US relations during the war, *Behind the Green Curtain*, in which belligerent internment is also addressed. Ralph Keefer's *Grounded in Eire* is another which deals with the experiences of Allied internees and, although it is based on the experiences of an internee in the Curragh who eventually escaped, it is effectively a work of fiction, filled with crude (and sometimes offensive) Irish stereotypes, unfeasibly snappy dialogue between the characters and overstated action sequences.[8]

The enduring narrative of the camp at K-Lines is one of an incongruous oasis in the middle of the European war, an oddity which could only happen in Ireland, where the internees whiled away their days in idle luxury, playing sport, drinking in pubs and enjoying the hospitality of the local population. The roots of this can be traced back to a series of articles in the *Toronto Star* newspaper in 1943, written by one of the internees, John Calder. In them, he described the belligerent internees as having an easy-going and indolent lifestyle;[9] his description of life in the camp was so laidback that it caused anger amongst some of his fellow Allied internees,[10] who were worried that they were being depicted as dodging

DOI: 10.1057/9781137446039.0003

the war. Calder's narrative has never truly been updated. More recently, British broadcaster Dan Snow depicted the internees' life as consisting of 'Fishing excursions, fox hunting, golf and trips to the pub in Naas'[11] while in 2013, the *Daily Express* described the Curragh as the 'cushiest POW camp' and 'some kind of Wonderland in which the Second World War had been reduced to a minor rivalry about which side of a pub to sit in'.[12] Even Robert Fisk, whose excellent book, *In Time of War*, remains a standard text on Irish neutrality and the Anglo-Irish relationship during the war, falls into the same trap, describing the Curragh as 'congenial' and a place that resembled a 'resort' rather than an internment camp.[13]

There is a much smaller body of literature concerning Irish men and women who were held captive by the Axis. The one work that is consistently quoted, as it remains the only book on the topic, is Robert Widders' *The Emperor's Irish Slaves: Prisoners of the Japanese in the Second World War*. This book makes little attempt to be impartial or objective and is written in a highly emotional tone. The author calculates that 650 Irish were prisoners of war in Asia,[14] but given the statistical anomalies present in other sections of the work, this figure cannot be relied upon. For example, Widders confidently states that four per cent of those Irish held as prisoners of war by Germany died in captivity;[15] however, a much more reliable source, Max Hastings, suggests that four percent of *all* British and American prisoners of war died while in German custody.[16] In 1945, the British government estimated that 1000 repatriated prisoners of war were from Ireland,[17] which suggests that Widders' figure for Irish prisoners in the Far East is too low. Unfortunately, the government document does not include a breakdown of whether these returning prisoners were in German or Japanese custody. One final odd feature of Widders' work is that he attempts to draw a bizarre and entirely inappropriate parallel between the payment of compensation to former prisoners of war by the British and Japanese governments in the 1950s, and a personal injuries case taken by an American woman against the McDonalds fast-food chain in 2011.[18] Of much more use to the researcher are the small but steadily growing body of Irish prisoner of war memoirs. While making use of literature, this work will concentrate on the Dublin government and its attempts to deal with the issues raised by military internees and prisoners of war, both inside and outside Ireland, rather than on individual prisoners or internees.

On a broader level, a study of this kind illustrates the de Valera government's difficulty in dealing with the war itself. As will be illustrated, in

DOI: 10.1057/9781137446039.0003

spite of the decision to remain neutral during the conflict, little preparatory work had been done before the outbreak of war either on belligerent internees or Irish prisoners of war. Despite repeated incursions into Irish airspace and several landings by British aircraft, it was not until the fall of France in June 1940 that the Irish government directed any serious attention towards its internment regime. Even then, the first internees were not detained until August 1940 and the crash of a Luftwaffe FW-200 in county Kerry sparked a debate on how they would be accommodated and the conditions they would live in, despite the war almost being a year old at that point. Likewise, regardless of the fact that Irish volunteers were streaming out of the country to join the British forces, no thought had been given to the consequences should they be captured, which would have an obvious impact on their families still in Ireland. Official positions on the despatch of parcels to prisoners of war or who was responsible for providing information to the relatives of Irish prisoners had not even been considered, and policy on issues such as these would be not set until well into the war. As a consequence, in dealing both with belligerent internees and Irish prisoners of war, the government consistently improvised throughout the war, sometimes adapting or copying British policies, or seeking advice from fellow neutral countries. While the attitude towards K-Lines became relatively consistent from 1942 onwards, the government's reaction to prisoners abroad was erratic.

Finally, Ireland's relationship with military internees and prisoners of war illustrates that while Eire was neutral, it was certainly not disconnected from the conflict. The de Valera government interacted constantly with representatives of the warring powers on issues regarding internment; de Valera himself attended conferences on the living conditions and parole arrangements for military internees. On several occasions, the German and British ministers in Dublin, seeking changes to the Irish internment system, directly approached him and the Department of External Affairs. Likewise, there was a constant flow of information between Dublin, the Red Cross and the belligerent countries as relatives and friends attempted to find information about Irish prisoners of war abroad, or send them letters and post. While discussing the question of Irish parcels for prisoners of war in 1943, the legal advisor to the Department of External Affairs, Michael Rynne emphasised just how complex Ireland's connection to the war was. He created a list of hypothetical recipients for prisoner packages sent from Ireland, including:

DOI: 10.1057/9781137446039.0003

An Englishman with Irish friends imprisoned in a German military camp (ii) an Irish lady with no passport, interned in France (iii) an Irish member of the New Zealand forces imprisoned in Italy (iv) an Irish mining engineer suspected of helping the British at Singapore in Japanese hands (v) a British officer in the Curragh (vi) a German civilian in Arbour Hill[19] (vii) a French (Vichy) military prisoner of War, with friends in Ireland (viii) a Jewish lady in the Isle of Man with relatives in the South Circular Road.[20]

Far from lurking in Plato's cave, to use FSL Lyons' pithy but now outdated phrase,[21] both the belligerent internee and the prisoner of war issue demonstrate that neutral Ireland was closely linked to the war.

Notes

1   Irish Military Archives, PM 633/733, 'History of Eire's Belligerent Camps', no date.

2   Irish Military Archives, C229A, letter from Liam O'hAodh, 17 December 1940.

3   J. Reynolds (2008) 'It's a Long Way to Tipperary: German POWs in Templemore' *History Ireland*, 16, 3, 23.

4   University College Cork, Volunteers Oral Archive, Tape A15, Denis Murnane.

5   S. Tanner (2000) *Refuge from the Reich: American Airmen and Switzerland during World War II* (New York: Sarpedon), p. 16.

6   R. Overy (2014) *The Bombing War: Europe 1939–1945* (London: Penguin), p. 373.

7   T.R. Dwyer (1994) *Guests of the State: The Story of Allied and Axis Servicemen Interned in Ireland during World War II* (Dingle: Brandon), p. 5.

8   R. Keefer (2002) *Grounded in Eire: The Story of Two RAF Fliers Interned in Ireland during World War II* (Montreal: McGill-Queen's University Press).

9   *Toronto Star*, 'Interned Canadian Fliers Live Life of Riley in Eire', 9 June 1943.

10 T.R. Dwyer (2010) *Behind the Green Curtain: Ireland's Phoney Neutrality during World War II* (Dublin: Gill and Macmillan), p. 260.

11 D. Snow (2011) 'Spitfire down: The WWII Camp Where Allies and Germans Mixed' [online] Available at: < http://www.bbc.co.uk/news/magazine-13924720> [Accessed 15 August 2013].

12 *Daily Express*, 'The Cushiest POW Camp', 7 November 2013.

13 R. Fisk (1985) *In Time of War: Ireland, Ulster and the Price of Neutrality, 1939–45* (Dublin: Gill & Macmillan), p. 177.

14 R. Widders (2012) *The Emperor's Irish Slaves: Prisoners of the Japanese in the Second World War* (Dublin: The History Press Ireland), p. 8.

15 Widders, *The Emperor's Irish Slaves*, p. 9.

16 M. Hastings (2007) *Nemesis: The Battle for Japan, 1944–45* (London: Harper Perennial), p. 374.

DOI: 10.1057/9781137446039.0003

17   National Archives of Ireland, DFA 341/11, Belton to Walshe, 5 December 1945.

18   Widders, *The Emperor's Irish Slaves*, p. 171.

19   Arbour Hill Prison, Dublin, was one location which was used to intern German agents sent to Ireland during the war.

20   National Archives of Ireland DFA 369/3, Rynne to Nolan 19 February 1943. The South Circular Road is in Dublin.

21   FSL Lyons (1986) *Ireland since the Famine* (London: Fontana Press), p. 558.

DOI: 10.1057/9781137446039.0003

1

Locking Them Up: Internment, Prisoners of War and International Law

Abstract: *One of the fundamental problems faced by the de Valera government when dealing with military internment during the Second World War was how to apply international law, such as the 1907 Hague and 1929 Geneva conventions, to the Irish situation.* Having had no previous experience of detaining belligerent personnel, neutral Ireland was initially content to apply international law to the internees, but moved away from this from 1942 onwards, when military internment was rooted in Irish emergency law, before circling back to international agreement in 1949. This chapter charts the evolution of Irish thinking on the legal basis of belligerent internment, as well as focusing on the way in which the internees were classified as prisoners, but not treated as such.

Keywords: emergency law; 1929 Geneva Convention; 1907 Hague Convention; international law; internment; prisoners of war

Kelly, Bernard. *Military Internees, Prisoners of War and the Irish State during the Second World War.* Basingstoke: Palgrave Macmillan, 2015. DOI: 10.1057/9781137446039.0004.

In a note to the Defence Forces Adjutant-General in August 1940, Colonel Liam Archer of G2 (Irish military intelligence) made a telling mistake. His letter concerned the conditions in which the first few German belligerent personnel were living in after being transferred to K-Lines and, when referring to them, Archer wrote 'German P.O.W.', which he then crossed out and replaced with 'internees'.[1] His confusion was understandable. The Irish government and military had no previous experience of detaining military personnel from other countries, and they had little idea how to classify them or how they were to be treated according to international law. Prior to the Second World War, the duties and obligations of neutral countries as regards the internment of belligerent personnel during wartime were set out in the 1907 Hague Convention. This stated that 'A neutral Power which receives on its territory troops belonging to the belligerent armies shall intern them, as far as possible, at a distance from the theatre of war', defining places of internment as camps, 'fortresses or in places set apart for this purpose'.[2] The experience of the First World War showed that this simple formulation was inadequate to deal with the complex question of over-flights and landings by belligerent aircraft in neutral countries. Dwight S. Meares has observed that between 1914 and 1918, some neutrals released belligerent aircrew if they had become lost during flight, as Norway did with a German airship crew in 1915, while others, such as Switzerland, often refused to do so.[3] In 1923, some clarity was brought to this issue when the General Report of the Hague Commission of Jurists upon the Revision of the Rules of Warfare categorically stated that a 'neutral government shall use the means at its disposal to intern any belligerent military aircraft which is within its jurisdiction after having alighted for any reason whatsoever, together with its crew and the passengers, if any'; however, it also suggested that neutral countries could make exceptions when belligerent aircraft were in distress, lost, experiencing engine difficulties or running out of fuel.[4]

Further regulations regarding the treatment of prisoners of war were laid out in the 1929 Geneva Convention Relative to the Treatment of Prisoners of War. Although Ireland signed the convention in July 1929, it did not ratify it, along with eight other countries such as Cuba, the Dominican Republic, Finland, Iran, Japan, Luxemburg, Nicaragua and Uruguay.[5] During the Second World War, the Japanese government announced that it would apply the 1929 convention to prisoners in its custody, but reserved the right to make exceptions for certain nationalities

DOI: 10.1057/9781137446039.0004

and races.[6] The duty of a neutral to detain belligerent personnel was reaffirmed in the 1939 Draft Convention on Rights and Duties of Neutral States in Naval and Aerial War'.[7] Thus, when the Second World War broke out in September 1939, there was a relatively firm legal framework instructing neutral states that they were under an obligation to intern members of belligerent forces but, crucially, there was little guidance on how to actually implement this policy, or how military internees were to be treated once detained.

Perhaps because of this, in the early part of the war, Dublin to all intents and purposes did not have an internment policy and was unprepared for the issue. No decision had been made on where or how belligerent personnel would be detained, or even if they would be. With British forces stationed in Northern Ireland, Irish members of the forces constantly circulating around Ireland on leave, thousands of reservists in the country and constant British air and naval activity around Ireland, it was clear that a firm internment policy would create significant difficulty for Dublin. If international rules were strictly enforced, Irish camps would rapidly fill up with personnel from the British and Commonwealth militaries, some of which would undoubtedly have been Irish themselves. During September 1939, several British seaplanes touched down in Irish waters and had extensive interactions with the local population and Gardaí; in one case, the pilot used the telephone in a Garda station[8] and in another a local mechanic helped repair the aircraft.[9] The government's lack of urgency reflected its attitude towards the war in general in this period. Despite declaring neutrality, preparations for the conflict were leisurely to say the least. For instance, the Defence Forces continued to recruit along peacetime lines: between 1 September 1939 and 31 May 1940, the army increased by 191 men and the reserve Volunteer Force only by 552.[10]

The one area in which the government acted relatively speedily was to move against the Irish Republican Army (IRA), which was known to have contacts with the German secret services. During the war, Berlin sent funds and 12 agents to Ireland to make contact with the IRA;[11] the majority of them were so hopelessly inept that they were captured within a few days or even hours. The most successful, Herman Goertz, spent 18 months on the run before being arrested in November 1941. The IRA had, somewhat farcically, declared war on Britain in January 1939; the subsequent bombing campaign on the British mainland was much more serious, killing seven and wounding 200.[12] This led to mounting pressure on the de Valera government to crack down on militant Irish republicans. Once war was declared, the Emergency Powers Act was passed by the Dáil and gave the de Valera government an extensive array of special powers. In December 1939 the IRA raided the Magazine Fort in the Phoenix Park, the Irish army's main munitions reserve, and escaped with around one million rounds of ammunition. As Colonel Dan Bryan of G2 noted after the war, the Magazine Fort raid was the 'Irish Pearl Harbour'[13] and afterwards the government moved decisively to suppress the IRA. After an early attempt to use the Special Criminal Court to detain republicans was struck down by the High Court, internment of republicans and IRA members under emergency law was introduced on 4 January 1940.[14] Internment under emergency legislation had the advantage, from the perspective of the government, of being exempt from judicial scrutiny[15] and No.1 internment camp at the Curragh was opened shortly afterwards, in May 1940. Republicans were also held at other locations such as Arbour Hill, Mountjoy and Portlaoise prisons. Over 1500 republican internees passed through the gates of Tintown, but the high level of transfers and releases meant that its highest monthly occupation was 547 in March 1943. Early in the war, the subject of the IRA and possible belligerent internments were connected by the Department of Defence; it noted that according to international guidelines shipwrecked sailors washing ashore in a neutral country would not necessarily have to be interned and it was feared that German agents would pose as distressed sailors to land in Eire, and subsequently attempt to join forces with the IRA. Defence urged the government to make a swift decision on belligerent service personnel, arguing that 'any course other than internment, possibly with the privilege of leaving the country within a stipulated period to avoid internment, may prove disastrous.'[16] In spite of this, little was done to prepare for the arrival of any potential belligerent internees.

The German attack on Western Europe in May 1940 and the unexpectedly swift fall of France in June forced a reappraisal of the belligerent internment policy. Writing on 24 June 1940, Michael Rynne, the legal advisor at the Department of External Affairs, suggested a radical new direction in Irish policy. He recommended that the porous border with Northern Ireland should be sealed off to prevent refugees from crossing, while members of the belligerent forces should also be apprehended:

> Whether these arrive over the Border, or by air and sea, they should be interned until the end of hostilities. This applies to land forces who may take refuge here having been routed in Ulster, to naval ratings shipwrecked

DOI: 10.1057/9781137446039.0004

on our shores and to airmen forced to land on our territory for any reason. Consequently, preparations should be made to accommodate internees in camps established as far as possible from the war zone.[17]

Rynne's attitude was a mixture of examples drawn from recent events in Europe and adherence to international law. The possibility that British forces would seek sanctuary in Eire after being 'routed in Ulster' was more than likely a reference to the Swiss practice in 1940 of interning French troops who crossed the Swiss border and sought asylum rather than surrender to the Germans.[18] At the same time, Rynne's memo reflected the main thrust of the 1907 Hague Convention, in particular its stipulation that belligerent internees be held at a safe distance from the combat area. His intervention came at a time when the focus of the war was shifting away from France towards Britain. The German air assault against Britain resulted in a surge of belligerent aircraft in and around Irish airspace, meaning that it was only a matter of time before one eventually made landfall. The Coast Watching Service reported that the number of belligerent aircraft observed jumped from 50 in April 1940 to 896 in August, of which 60 were spotted inland.[19]

De Valera was forced into formulating a clear stance on belligerent internment on 20 August 1940, when a Luftwaffe FW-200 Condor crashed on a mountainside in county Kerry. The crew of six were taken into custody, given medical treatment in Cork and Tralee before eventually being transported to the Curragh. Following on from his advice in June, Rynne wrote on 21 August that the Hague Convention regarding prisoners of war was 'now generally believed to be appropriate to the treatment of internees, members of the belligerent forces who fell into the hands of a neutral', therefore 'it seems sufficiently clear that we must intern German crew of the bomber which has just been forced to land in Kerry'.[20] The papers of Colonel Dan Bryan also illustrate that this was the turning point in Irish internment policy: the Coastal and Aerial Intelligence section noted that 'Since August all belligerent airmen landing in our territory have been interned'.[21] Before the Germans crashed in Kerry on 20 August, no preparations had been made to house belligerent internees. A list of possible internment camp locations in the Irish military archives is dated 22 August 1940 and contains a mixture of castles and large houses,[22] some of which were owned by former members of the British military. The final order from Liam O'hAodh, the military Adjutant-General, to transfer the men to K-Lines was made nine days after the Germans crash-landed.[23]

DOI: 10.1057/9781137446039.0004

Furthermore, it was clear that the government, despite having almost a full year to prepare for the eventuality, had no idea how to actually treat these men once they were incarcerated. For advice, de Valera turned to Dr Richard Hayes, the Director of the National Library and advisor to G2, who on 31 August noted that

> When considering the form, place and conditions of internment it should be noted that international law does not make a distinction between prisoners of war captured by a belligerent and armed forces of a belligerent interned by a neutral. It is clear from the Hague Conventions of 1907 that "internees" if not "prisoners of war" are in the same position as "prisoners of war" and that, mutatis mutandis, the rules governing the treatment of each class are the same. In the case of "prisoners of war", the belligerent capturing them does not want them to return to his enemy's forces and so detains them forcibly. In the case of internees, the neutral is under an obligation imposed on him by the duty of impartiality not to permit the internees to rejoin their own forces. The motives for detention are different in each case but the duty to detain and the method of detainment are the same.
>
> We can therefore regard internees in all matters in the position of "prisoners of war". This enables us to apply to them the rules laid down in the Hague Convention of 1907 except in so far as they have been modified by the International Convention relative to the Treatment of Prisoners of War, Geneva, 1929.[24]

This opinion was founded on solid European precedent. In April 1940 the International Red Cross, recognizing that there were no regulations on how military internees were to be treated by neutral countries, wrote to all European neutrals urging them to apply the 1929 prisoner of war provisions to belligerent internees.[25] This was adopted by most states, but both Sweden and Switzerland protested against this. Switzerland in particular argued that the extension of prisoner of war regulations to military internees was in itself a breach of international law[26] and all through the conflict belligerent personnel in Switzerland were subject to Swiss national law.

However, the stance taken by the Red Cross was accepted by most other neutrals and also by the United States once it entered the war in December 1941. The US Legation in Switzerland argued that American internees were 'in a position analogous to that of prisoners of war'.[27] Hayes' advice to the Irish government was similar to Rynne's in June; both were content to frame the internment policy within the parameters set by international law and argued that treating belligerent internees

DOI: 10.1057/9781137446039.0004

as prisoners of war allowed Dublin to extend the full protection of the Hague Convention to them. Despite the fact that they were classed as prisoners, they were never *treated* as such, apart for a very brief period in September–October 1940. Applying international agreements to belligerent internees allowed the Irish government to establish a baseline on how to treat the service personnel: what standard of food to provide, what liability the State had to provide clothes and medical treatment to them. In addition, as the document did not actually refer to internees in neutral countries, it was up to Dublin how far to apply it to them. As Rynne wrote in May 1942, the convention provided 'very valuable criterion' in dealing with military internees and the government should view it as a flexible structure upon which to build its own distinct policy. As he noted

> We cannot go far wrong if we (1) reject the provisions which imply hardship on the interned men ... and (2) apply generously those provisions which endeavor to protect the welfare of the detained persons.[28]

'For "prisoner of war" in the Convention', he wrote a fortnight later, 'one must always read "internee."'[29] Both he and Hayes were in agreement that, although prisoner of war conventions could be applied to them, military internees were not actually prisoners.

However, the initial classification as prisoners briefly affected the lives of the early internees. The Irish military controlled the camp and the prisoners were guarded by the Irish Defence Forces Póilíní Airm (PA: military police). The Irish military felt that the internees needed to be held under very heavy security, a situation which lasted until October 1940, when *de facto* control of the camp passed from the Department of Defence to the Department of External Affairs. This was done in order to allow the government more flexibility in handling the diplomatic aspects of internment, and the restrictions on the internees were eased considerably. Hayes' judgment on how they could be classified was also quite prescient. The 1949 Geneva Convention on Prisoners of War stated that belligerent internees in neutral countries were to be treated as well as prisoners of war were. However, as an Irish review of the 1949 Convention noted in 1954, belligerent internees were not to be officially classified as prisoners, but that their conditions of internment could not be worse than prisoners of war in belligerent countries.[30]

The issue of Irish prisoners of war in Axis custody was much clearer for the de Valera government. Dublin had neither legal standing nor

DOI: 10.1057/9781137446039.0004

any power to intervene on behalf of Irish members of the Allied forces, prisoners or otherwise. In March 1940, External Affairs declined to help an Irish family secure their son's release from the New Zealand Expeditionary Force; assistant secretary of the department Frederick Boland wrote that

> Our general practice in this type of case shd. be based on the principle that Irish citizens who have enrolled themselves in, and made themselves subject to the discipline of, foreign armed forces cannot look to the Irish Govt. for diplomatic protection or assistance against the military authorities to whom they have become subject in relation to matters connected with their service.[31]

In a similar vein, responding to a letter from an Irish member of the Women's Auxiliary Air Force (WAAF) in September 1942, the secretary of the Department of External Affairs, Joseph Walshe, noted that although her status as a citizen of Eire remained unchanged by her joining the British forces, she 'may be regarded as having voluntarily relinquished Irish diplomatic protection by enrolling in the W.A.A.F.'.[32] In 1943, two Irish members of the British forces who had been arrested after crossing illegally into Spain contacted the Irish Legation. They were held in the camp at Miranda de Ebro, where all foreigners who had escaped German occupied Europe and arrested in Spain were detained. Generally, British troops who were sent here were detained only for a number of weeks before arrangements could be made for their repatriation.[33] Although Michael Rynne at External Affairs was of the opinion that the Irish Legation had a duty to help the men,[34] the government declined to assist them. In an interesting example of how the military internees in the Curragh had an effect on Irish prisoners overseas, the Irish attitude towards the men in Spain was derived from the experience of the lone American in K-Lines. Roland Wolfe, a volunteer in the RAF, crashed in Ireland in late 1941 and was interned; because he was in the British forces, all correspondence and contact regarding his case came through the British authorities. As Boland noted, when he escaped from the Curragh in December 1941 in dubious circumstances, it was the British and not the Americans who decided to return him to Irish custody,[35] and this provided Dublin with a useful precedent to use. The official reply to the Madrid Legation stated that

> The diplomatic protection of Irish citizens, who have served in the British Forces, does not fall upon the Irish Representatives abroad and we have

DOI: 10.1057/9781137446039.0004

observed that, as between the British and American authorities here, diplomatic protection of members of the R.A.F., who are American citizens, rests with the British authorities.[36]

In the case of Irish prisoners in the British forces, any interventions had to be made either by the International Red Cross or by Switzerland, which was the protecting power of both German and British prisoners of war.[37] On one occasion, de Valera attempted to prevent the execution of an Irish prisoner of war, who had escaped the destruction of his British unit in France during 1940 and was eventually captured in civilian clothes by the Germans after attempting to rob a French inn during April 1942. Joseph Walshe sent a message to the Irish Legation in Berlin, asking that they 'Do everything possible to have sentence remitted.'[38] The Legation contacted the German authorities directly and found that the Swiss, as protecting power, had already been dealing with the issue. The death sentence was eventually revoked, but it is unlikely that this was because of the involvement of Dublin; the Swiss Legation told their Irish counterparts in Berlin that 'no prisoner of war condemned to death has been executed'.[39] The lack of influence Ireland had was shown by the fact that Dublin relied almost entirely on the Swiss for information regarding the prisoner, and could do little for him.

When contacted by Martin Brennan, a Fianna Fáil TD for Sligo, regarding a possible exchange of prisoners of war, Joseph Walshe replied that any 'exchange would be entirely a matter for the country in whose Armed Forces he was serving at the time of his capture, and the Irish government would have no locus standi in this matter'.[40] Once Japan entered the war in December 1941, matters became more complicated. Ireland had no diplomatic presence in the Far East and had traditionally relied on Britain for its consular activities in the region. After Britain and Japan went to war, Walshe instructed the Irish minister in Lisbon, Colman O'Donovan, to ask the Portuguese government to take over Britain's role on Ireland's behalf.[41] With Irish civilians, mostly religious missionaries, scattered all over Asia, Dublin was keen to maintain a relationship with Tokyo, but this was fraught with difficulty. For instance, in 1943 the raising of the Japanese consulate in Dublin to a consulate-general provoked a sharp enquiry from David Gray, US minister in Dublin, and a telegram from US Secretary of State Cordell Hull, asking for confirmation of 'the extension of this gratuitous courtesy to our enemy'.[42]

DOI: 10.1057/9781137446039.0004

Throughout the war, when the families of Irish members of the British forces, either missing or confirmed to be prisoners, contacted the government seeking information, they received a variety of responses; again illustrating that there was no pre-prepared policy. The most common one was a referral to the Irish, British or International Red Cross, or the Prisoner of War Department of the British government. On some occasions, the government undertook to contact the Swiss government to enquire about Irish prisoners and in these cases, External Affairs usually asked the enquirer to forward a cheque to cover the cost of the telegrams; for instance, on 10 February 1941, External Affairs requested a deposit of £1.10.[43]

During 1940 and into 1941, there was still concern in government circles over the shallow legal foundation of the belligerent internment policy. The matter was first mentioned during an External Affairs and Defence joint conference in February 1941. It was Frederick Boland himself who raised it, stating that there were 'no specified powers' in relation to belligerent internment and that 'in view of the numbers of the internees, the possibility of the legal position being challenged cannot be overlooked'.[44] In December 1941 a Department of Defence memo pointed out that, while the warring powers were unlikely to challenge Eire's right to detain belligerent personnel, 'It is not, however, outside the bounds of possibility, in the peculiar circumstances of this country, than an effort might be made, otherwise than by the Powers themselves, to obtain the release of internees by way of habeas corpus proceedings'.[45] The 'peculiar circumstances' referred to were the tens of thousands of Eire citizens then currently serving in the Allied forces, particularly the British. Interning an Irish member of the Allied forces could lead to potentially severe legal problems and a successful challenge to their internment could call the whole system into question. If Dublin was forced to either abandon its internment policy or to enforce it strictly as a result of a successful challenge, the resulting lack of control could have led to problematic relationships with the belligerents. There was a relatively recent precedent for this: in 1926 an Irish deserter from the British army successfully opposed his deportation from the Irish Free State, and the then Attorney-General, John A. Costello, found in favour of the soldier on the grounds that he had not broken any Irish law.[46] Theoretically, any Irish member of the Allied forces could use the same argument if interned from 1940 onwards, and the Attorney-General was of the opinion that even an official arrest warrant signed by the Minister

DOI: 10.1057/9781137446039.0004

for Justice was unlikely to survive in court.[47] Although it was felt that such a challenge was unlikely, de Valera himself thought 'it well to ensure against such a contingency by providing for internment under our own municipal law'.[48] This marked the first move in a decisive shift away from international guidelines and towards Irish law. The nightmare scenario of an Irish member of the Allied forces crashing in Eire actually occurred in July 1942, when an RAF aircraft made landfall in Donegal, carrying an Irish crewmember who was, ironically, a native of Donegal. He and his crew were quickly spirited to the border with Northern Ireland.[49] Robert Fisk has reported that another such incident took place during 1943. In this case, an RAF Sunderland flying boat crashed in county Kerry; one of the crew, a man from Limerick, was permitted to visit his home before they were transported to the border.[50]

One possible alternative that was considered was to arrest all belligerent personnel under Emergency Powers Order (EPO) no. 20. There was some sense in this suggestion, as German agents sent to Ireland had been interned under this order, as well as members of the IRA.[51] However, this order was aimed at those who were deemed a severe danger to the state and, as Frederick Boland said, the need to intern belligerent personnel arose from 'the sincere desire of the State to carry out its international obligations as a neutral' rather than any suggestion that the men in K-Lines threatened the stability of the country.[52] Another drawback of this solution was that under EPO no. 20, belligerent personnel would be subjected to the full rigours of political internment, including being fingerprinted and having their photographs taken, which was hardly likely to help the morale of the camp. Measures such as these were similar to what prisoners of war in Europe went through after capture[53] and were likely to trigger complaints from the warring nations.

The most obvious solution was that favoured by de Valera: to move away from international law and draw up a new Emergency Powers Order specifically dealing with belligerent personnel, but which would firmly anchor their internment in current emergency law. Such an approach meant that there would be no complex debates over interpretations of international conventions, and the government would have a clear legal basis for their actions, but it also presented its own problems. At any given time, Ireland was host to hundreds of Irish members of the British forces home on leave, as well as other Allied troops who travelled to Dublin regularly, and any blanket internment order would automatically apply to them as well. To get around this, it was suggested that only

DOI: 10.1057/9781137446039.0004

belligerent personnel arriving in Eire while in uniform should be subject to internment. This meant that EPO no. 17, signed in October 1939 and 'devised to prevent the wearing of British uniforms in this State'[54] had to be amended. The Department of Defence suggested that the British military be requested to provide civilian clothes to any Irish personnel coming home on leave.[55] They seemed to be unaware that de Valera had already raised this issue with Sir John Maffey, the UK Representative in Eire, as early as October 1939,[56] and that Maffey had promised to take measures to restrict the practice.[57]

It has been suggested in other works (my own included) that the de Valera government banned the wearing of British uniforms in Ireland in October 1939 as a way of disguising the extent of Irish participation in the British forces, or as a way of maintaining the façade of neutrality.[58] While there remains a great deal of truth in this, the complex debate over belligerent internment and the uniform issue shows that, to some extent at least, the government needed Irish members of the British forces to wear civilian clothes in order to avoid interning them, and specifically altered the proposed Emergency Powers Order to accommodate them.

Eventually, the government drew up two emergency orders dealing with belligerent internment. The first, EPO no. 170, gave ministers the power to intern anyone if it was 'expedient in the interests of the preservation of the State', but it was careful to note that the order was linked to 'the international obligations of the State'; this differentiated the belligerent internees from the republican detainees in No.1 camp and undercover Axis agents apprehended while in Eire. Rather than rely on the 1907 Hague Convention to decide where belligerents could be held, EPO no. 170 passed that authority to the Minister for Defence, who had the final say over the 'places, manner and conditions of internment'.[59] As a result of its introduction, on 1 May 1942 Minister for Defence Oscar Traynor signed an order for the internment of 32 British and Commonwealth personnel already in custody,[60] as well as the German personnel. From that point on, a signed directive from Traynor accompanied all new arrivals in K-Lines. The second was EPO no. 171, which concerned assistance given to internees to escape. It became an offence to help internees escape, to harbour them after escape or to assist them to leave the State. It applied both to civilians outside the wire and internees within the camp who aided their comrades to break out. Entering an internment camp without authorisation was also prohibited, as was interfering with the administration of the camp, smuggling correspondence for any internee or conveying any

DOI: 10.1057/9781137446039.0004

'article of food (including confectionary), or any liquid, cigars, cigarettes, or tobacco, or any money, securities, jewellery or like valuable articles, or any articles capable of facilitating the escape of an interned person.'

After the war, when the new Inter-Party government was discussing Ireland's signing the 1949 Geneva Convention, the Attorney-General warned that, if the government signed the document, it would have some consequences if Ireland found itself neutral in a future war and had to again intern belligerent personnel. 'We were not bound in the matter by Convention in the last world war', the Attorney-General admitted, 'and the method of partly shelving and partly compromising which we adopted could not be repeated on our becoming parties to the new Convention.'[61]

Ireland signed the Convention 'without reservations' in December 1949, which meant that Dublin needed to alter aspects of Irish law to come into line with the Convention. In particular, the conditions in which any future belligerent internees would be held in had to be set out in Irish law, along the lines of the Convention. As well as that, the link between the two groups was made explicit: 'the term "prisoners of war" includes members of the belligerent armed forces who might be interned here during a war in which this country was neutral'.[62] The legislation was finally signed into law as the 'Prisoners of war and enemy aliens act, 1956', which gave the Minister for Defence or any other Minister the power to intern prisoners of war of any or a single nationality, or any particular category of prisoner of war.[63]

Conclusion

The signing of the 1949 Convention and its eventual implementation through Irish law meant that the situation during the Second World War, in which the Dublin government picked which aspects of international internment regulations it wished to follow, could not occur again. The legal basis of the Irish military internment regime during the Second World War, an improvised mixture of international law and emergency decree, was therefore unique in Irish history. Although Dublin never again arrested and detained members of foreign military forces during wartime, from 1956 onwards it was bound into the international legal system. The experiment of 1940–46, of partially implementing and partially ignoring international law, could not be repeated.

DOI: 10.1057/9781137446039.0004

Notes

1   Irish Military Archives, S/231, Archer to Adjutant-General, 31 August 1940.

2   International Committee of the Red Cross, https://www.icrc.org/applic/ihl/ ihl.nsf/Article.xsp?key=fortresses&action=openDocument&documentId=3C 5ACCA7CF58497CC12563CD00516A15, date accessed 28 November 2014.

3   D.S. Meares (2013) 'Neutral States and the Application of International Law to United States Airmen during World War II. To Intern or Not to Intern?' *Journal of the History of International Law*, 15, 81–82.

4   O.J. Lissitzyn (1953) 'The Treatment of Aerial Intruders in Recent Practice and International Law', *The American Journal of International Law*, 47, 4, 563.

5   International Committee of the Red Cross, https://www.icrc.org/applic/ ihl/ihl.nsf/States.xsp?xp_viewStates=XPages_NORMStatesSign&xp_ treatySelected=305, date accessed 28 November 2014.

6   B. MacArthur (2005) *Surviving the Sword: Prisoners of the Japanese in the Far East, 1942–45* (New York: Random House), p. 48.

7   Meares, 'Neutral States and the Application of International Law', 82.

8   T.R. Dwyer (1994) *Guests of the State: The Story of Allied and Axis Servicemen Interned in Ireland during World War II* (Dingle: Brandon Press), p. 11.

9   Dwyer, *Guests of the State*, p. 12.

10 Irish Military Archives, *General Commentary on the Emergency Period Part I: General Commentary*, p. 14.

11 E. O'Halpin (2000) *Defending Ireland: The Irish State and Its Enemies since 1922* (Oxford: Oxford University Press), p. 240.

12 H. Patterson (2007) *Ireland since 1939: The Persistence of Conflict* (London: Penguin), p. 54.

13 University College Dublin Archives, Dan Bryan papers, P71/101, 'IRA', undated research notes.

14 M. Walsh (2010) *G2 In Defence of Ireland: Irish Military Intelligence 1918–45* (Cork: The Collins Press), p. 142.

15 D. Keogh and M. O'Driscoll (2004) *Ireland in World War Two: Neutrality and Survival* (Cork: Mercier Press), p. 66.

16 Irish Military Archives, S/231, undated Defence memo.

17 *Documents on Irish Foreign Policy, Volume VI*, p. 262.

18 D.F. Vagts (1997) 'Switzerland, International Law and World War II', *American Journal of International Law*, 91, 3, 467.

19 University College Dublin Archives, Dan Bryan papers, P71/32, 'Coastal and Aerial Intelligence Section', undated.

20 Irish Military Archives, S/231, memo by Michael Rynne, 21 August 1940.

21 University College Dublin Archives, Dan Bryan papers, P71/32, 'Coastal and Aerial Intelligence Section', undated.

DOI: 10.1057/9781137446039.0004

22 Irish Military Archives, S/231, 'Unoccupied premises which might be suitable for certain purposes', 22 August 1940.

23 Irish Military Archives, S/231, letter from Liam O'hAodh to O/C Southern Command, 29 August 1940.

24 Irish Military Archives, S/231, memo by Richard Hayes, 31 August 1940.

25 D.S. Meares (2013) 'Better off as Prisoners of War. The Differential Standard of Protection for Military Internees in Switzerland during World War II', *Journal of the History of International Law*, 15, 175–76.

26 Mears, 'Better off as Prisoners of War', 190.

27 Tanner, *Refuge from the Reich*, p. 150.

28 National Archives of Ireland, DFA 241/309, Rynne to Boland, 4 May 1942.

29 National Archives of Ireland, DFA 241/309, Rynne to Boland, 14 May 1942.

30 National Archives of Ireland, AGO 2003/4/340 'International Law Red Cross Prisoners of War and enemy aliens', 'Obligations of neutral states in relation to the internment of members of the Belligerent Forces', 1954.

31 National Archives of Ireland, DFA 241/151 'Release of Irish Nationals from the armed Forces of the Dominions', Boland to Belton, 31 May 1940.

32 National Archives of Ireland, DFA 241/334 'Enquiry as to the position of Irish persons in the British forces in the event of Ireland's entry into the war on the side of Germany', letter from Walshe, 9 September 1942.

33 M. Eiroa and C. Pallarés (2014) 'Uncertain Fates: Allied Soldiers at the Miranda de Ebro Concentration Camp', *The Historian*, 76, 1, 38.

34 National Archives of Ireland, DFA 241/364, Rynne to Nolan, 16 March 1943.

35 National Archives of Ireland, DFA 241/364, note by Boland, 19 March 1943.

36 National Archives of Ireland, DFA 241/364, Fay to Madrid, 31 March 1943.

37 Vagts, 'Switzerland, International Law and World War II', 471.

38 National Archives of Ireland, DFA 241/127/12, telegram from Walshe, 29 October 1943.

39 National Archives of Ireland, DFA DFA 241/127/12, telegram from Irish Legation Berlin, 11 July 1944.

40 National Archives of Ireland, DFA 241/392 'Enquiry re the exchange of Prisoners of War', Walshe to Brennan 19 November 1943.

41 *Documents on Irish Foreign Policy, Volume VII*, p. 174.

42 National Archives of Ireland, DFA 318/104, telegram from Hull, 4 June 1943.

43 National Archives of Ireland, DFA 241/127, letter from Nolan, 10 February 1941.

44 Irish Military Archives, S/231 'Conference – Internment – Department of Defence', conference 1 February 1941.

45 National Archives of Ireland, TAOIS S 12094A, draft memo for government, December 1941. Underline in the original.

46 B. Kelly (2012) 'British Military Deserters in the Irish Free State, 1922–1932.' *Studia Hibernica*, 38, 209.

DOI: 10.1057/9781137446039.0004

47   National Archives of Ireland, TAOIS S 12094A, minutes of a conference at the Attorney-General's office, 26 January 1942.

48   National Archives of Ireland, TAOIS S 12094A, 'internment of members of belligerent armed forces', draft memo for government, December 1941.

49   Dwyer, *Guests of the State*, p. 113.

50   R. Fisk (1985) *In Time of War: Ireland, Ulster and the Price of Neutrality, 1939–1945* (Dublin: Gill & Macmillan), p. 329.

51   National Archives of Ireland, JUS 8/944, 'Estimates 1945–6'

52   National Archives of Ireland, TAOIS S 12094A, minutes of a conference at the Attorney-General's office, 26 January 1942.

53   M. Gillies (2011) *The Barbed Wire University: The Real Lives of Allied Prisoners of War in the Second World War* (London: Aurum), p. 17.

54   National Archives of Ireland, JUS 90/119/316, letter from Beary, 17 October 1941.

55   National Archives of Ireland, JUS 90/119/316, Beary to Walshe, 3 November 1941.

56   B. Girvin (2006) *The Emergency: Neutral Ireland, 1939–1945* (London: Macmillan), p. 277.

57   National Archives of Ireland, DFA 241/95, letter from Maffey, 2 November 1939.

58   B. Kelly (2012) *Returning Home: Irish Ex-Servicemen after the Second World War* (Dublin: Merrion Press), pp. 158–59.

59   National Archives of Ireland, JUS 90/119/316, Emergency Powers (no. 170) Order, 1942.

60   Irish Military Archives, PM 633, List signed by Traynor, 1 May 1942.

61   National Archives of Ireland, AGO 2003/4/340 'International Law Red Cross Prisoners of War and enemy aliens', undated memo.

62   National Archives of Ireland, TAOIS S 15366 'Ratification of the International Convention of the Protection of War Victims as signed at Geneva in 1949', 14 June 1952.

63   Irish Statute Book, http://www.irishstatutebook.ie/1956/en/act/pub/0027/print.html#sec4, date accessed 28 November 2014.

2

Keeping One Eye Abroad: Belligerent Internment and Diplomacy

Abstract: *This chapter explores the difficulty that the Irish government had in combining two increasingly divergent objectives: fulfilling its international obligations as a neutral, and maintaining its crucial relationships with the Allies. From the very beginning of the war, Irish neutrality and the internment regime was orientated towards Britain, a trend which became much more pronounced once America entered the conflict. Dublin consistently prioritised the maintenance of good relations with the Allies, and demonstrated this by releasing Allied aircraft and crew which crashed on Irish territory, while simultaneously interning all Germans who landed in Ireland. It further shows that Ireland was not alone in tailoring its internment regimes towards the Allies, and that all European neutrals compromised in their internment policies.*

Keywords: Allies; American; non-operational; operational; release

Kelly, Bernard. *Military Internees, Prisoners of War and the Irish State during the Second World War.* Basingstoke: Palgrave Macmillan, 2015. DOI: 10.1057/9781137446039.0005.

In 1945, the Dominions Office in London drew up a document which listed 19 ways in which the government of neutral Ireland had assisted Britain during the war. Alongside matters such as allowing Allied aircraft to cut across Donegal to reach the Atlantic, the supply of Irish meteorological data and the constant flow of Irish recruits for the British forces, the Dominions Office noted that the de Valera government had agreed to intern all German personnel who landed in Ireland, while they negotiated the eventual release of all Allied personnel in the Curragh. Later added to the list was the fact that 'Since 1941 all force-landed Allied aircraft have been allowed to take off again if airworthy and have been refuelled and otherwise assisted by the Eire Air Corps as necessary for this purpose. All damaged force-landed Allied aircraft are now salvaged by the Eire Air Corps and returned by them to the RAF authorities at the Northern Ireland border'.[1] Most of these aircraft and personnel were handed over at the border at the towns of Pettigo and Belleek on the borderline between Donegal and Fermanagh. The Pettigo-Belleek area had been the scene of a firefight between Irish troops, British army and Royal Ulster Constabulary (RUC) in June 1922, which threatened to become a major Anglo-Irish crisis, and it is therefore somewhat ironic that it was this area the eventually became the conduit for intense military cooperation between the former adversaries. The Dominions Office list illustrated that the Irish internment policy was closely tied to Dublin's neutrality. As the war went on and Irish neutrality became increasingly pro-Allied, so too did the belligerent internment policy. Robert Fisk has highlighted the shift in the Irish government's attitude towards internment as marking the period when Dublin moved from friendly to 'benevolent' neutrality,[2] particularly after America entered the war. Relations between Dublin and the Allies were difficult at times during the conflict. Churchill's well-known and often-expressed irritation with Irish neutrality aside, there were several other areas of disagreement. De Valera's refusal to allow British access to Irish ports throughout 1940, his intervention to prevent the introduction of conscription in Northern Ireland in 1939 and again in 1941, his protest at the landing of US troops in the province in 1942 and his rejection of the demand to expel Axis diplomats in February 1944 (known in Irish history as the American Note crisis) were all flashpoints in the Irish-Allied relationship throughout the war. Interpreting its internment obligations in a way which was advantageous towards the Allies was one way to reduce the tension and Robert Fisk has even suggested that the liberal concessions offered to

DOI: 10.1057/9781137446039.0005

the Allies over downed aircrew is an example of Irish 'collusion' with the Allies.[3] In large part, Irish neutrality relied on the restraint on the part of Britain and the US,[4] both of which had the military and economic power to cripple Eire if they wished. A liberal approach to belligerent internment was part of a larger policy of covert cooperation to ensure that this restraint continued.

The connection between internment and neutrality operated on three levels. The first was visible from the opening days of the war: the in-built bias within Irish neutrality towards Britain was replicated in the lack of any internment policy once the conflict broke out. There were few, if any, German aircraft in Irish skies in the early period of the war; the absence of any intention to intern downed pilots therefore exclusively assisted Britain. Even after mid-1940, when Dublin was forced to implement a much more evenly balanced regime, considerable leeway was still granted to British aircraft which landed in Eire. Secondly, Dublin was susceptible to pressure from the belligerents because of conditions with the internment camp itself. Because the Axis and Allied internees had direct and unsupervised access to their diplomatic representatives, any dissatisfaction with life inside K-Lines could quickly be translated into pressure on the Dublin government. The initially strict conditions within the camp were transformed after representations from the German minister in Dublin, Eduard Hempel in late 1940. The importance attached by de Valera to the diplomatic aspects of internment was reinforced when, in October 1940, the Department of External Affairs took over the leading role in running K-Lines, effectively removing responsibility from the Department of Defence. Finally, alterations in the internment policy were a way of reaching out directly to the belligerents, in particular the United States. De Valera's decision not to intern any American personnel, regardless of the circumstances of their arrival in Eire, is the best illustration of this. From 1942 until the end of the war, 39 American aircraft landed in neutral Ireland; the 275 surviving personnel were all released.[5] RAF pilot Roland Wolfe remained the only American incarcerated in K-Lines.

The concessions granted to the Allies, both inside and outside the camp, created a ripple effect within the internment policy, which gradually whittled away Dublin's position. Once it became clear that Dublin was exempting US aircrew from internment, the UK representative, Sir John Maffey, pressed for the same consideration to be given to British personnel; when this was granted in October 1943, leading to the release

DOI: 10.1057/9781137446039.0005

of some interned men, pressure was then applied to have Allied personnel exempted from internment completely. This was effectively agreed by de Valera in June 1944, when all remaining Allied internees were removed and released, while German sailors and aircrew who continued to land in Eire were all interned, right up to the very end of the war. Arguably from 1942, certainly from 1944 onwards, Dublin was openly and consciously operating internment against Germany only, a position which had its roots in the early leniency shown to Britain and the US in internment decisions.

From the very beginning of the war, Irish neutrality was closely linked to Dublin's relationship with Britain. On 25 August 1939, secretary of External Affairs Joseph Walshe penned a memo for his minister, de Valera. With war on the continent inevitable, Walshe laid out the foundations of the Irish stance towards the conflict for de Valera, for the Taoiseach to pass onto the German representative in Dublin. 'Our position vis-à-vis the European conflict is that of a neutral State', wrote Walshe, but the situation was not as simple as that. 'Our neutrality', he continued, 'cannot have all the characters of those neutral States which have had a long existence as separate States.' The Irish economy was still intimately bound up with the British and Ireland's strategic position, sitting astride the major Atlantic trade routes, meant that a certain consideration for Britain had to be built into Irish neutrality. In particular, the Irish government had to ensure that Ireland would never be used as a base from which to attack Britain and 'Any such activities directed against our powerful neighbour would ipso facto constitute a menace to our existence as a separate State'. This attitude pre-dated the war by several years: de Valera publicly stated in the Dáil in May 1935 that the overriding defence priority of his government was to prevent any other country striking at Britain through Ireland.[6] Dublin warned that Irish neutrality would inevitably be closely tied to Britain and Walshe suggested that if Germany was unable to accept this, then the two countries should withdraw their respective Legations.[7]

The same lenient approach to Britain was visible in the internment policy in the early days of the war. As already noted, several British aircraft touched down in Ireland or in Irish waters, and all were allowed to leave, sometimes after being repaired or refuelled. Likewise, Walshe visited British Foreign Secretary Anthony Eden on 7 September 1939 and – in an obvious attempt to quash the rumours that U-boats were using the west coast of Ireland as refuges – told Eden that Ireland 'intended to

DOI: 10.1057/9781137446039.0005

intern any crews of German submarines who might be obliged to land on our shores'.[8] This same point was repeated in a note to the British, French and German governments on 12 September.[9]

During October 1939, Colonel Liam Archer of G2 suggested to Walshe that the threat of internment be used to extract concessions in talks with the British government: unless London clamped down on false newspaper stories about covert Irish aid to Germany, then 'we will be absolutely compelled to intern the next British aircraft and crew that may fall into our hands', implying that Dublin had been deliberate in its leniency, an attitude which continued well into 1940. In May, an RAF Hampden landed by mistake at the Curragh camp and, despite having been in action over Germany, it was refuelled and allowed to leave.[10] Indeed, despite these early landings, the first British pilot did not see the inside of the Curragh until the end of September 1940, and his lightly-damaged Hurricane was bought from the RAF and became part of the Irish Air Corps. However, even after this, when Dublin had committed to interning all belligerent personnel who landed in Ireland, exceptions were still made for the British. In December 1940, two British sailors were arrested in Donegal but were then released over the border; an action that, even in the opinion of the British, probably breached neutrality.[11] Michael Kennedy has further noted that in the early days of the Coast Watching Service, established to monitor air and sea traffic in and around Irish waters and airspace, the lack of training worked to British advantage. Coast watchers were initially unable to distinguish between British and German aircraft; the result, as Maffey noted, was that aircraft were excluded from coast watching reports and thus the RAF, which was the dominant presence in Irish skies, could over-fly Eire without fear of recognition.[12] This situation was gradually improved and the Coast Watching Service became extremely proficient in tracking and recording both Allied and Axis incursions into Irish airspace.

The early internees in K-Lines lived under intense military security and were guarded so closely that it sparked a complaint from the German minister in Dublin. Initial responsibility for the camp rested with the Department of Defence and with Colonel Thomas McNally, officer commanding of Curragh Command, with responsibility for both the republican detainees in No.1 camp and the belligerent personnel in No.2 camp. Guards rotated duties between the two camps and it was inevitable that some of the antagonism between the PAs and the IRA would transfer from Tintown to K-Lines. Following a visit to the camp,

DOI: 10.1057/9781137446039.0005

Hempel contacted External Affairs in September 1940 to complain about the tight security and the general conditions the German internees lived in. Among the specific issues he identified were: they were not allowed to drink alcohol, they had no wireless set or newspapers, and they had not been issued with civilian clothes and so were still wearing the uniforms they had been captured in. Even IRA internees, when they needed them, were issued with civilian clothes at the State's expense,[13] which they were permitted to keep when released. Hempel further pointed out that while the men were being treated in hospital, their windows had been nailed shut and they were deprived of fresh air; in short, as the senior German officer, Oberleutnant Kurt Mollenhauer, commented to Hempel, they 'seemed to be regarded as prisoners of war rather than as military internees'. He hoped that the restrictions would be loosened, that Mollenhauer would be allowed to visit the German Legation in Dublin, and that all the internees would be allowed to practice their civilian occupations, as amongst the aircrew were mechanics, a gardener and a student.[14]

Although the complaint was delivered in a friendly manner, assistant secretary of External Affairs Frederick Boland at External Affairs took it extremely seriously and contacted Defence urging that the restrictions be reduced. He argued that while it was Dublin's duty as a neutral to intern these men, it was futile to make their incarceration unbearable. 'There is no point whatever', Boland wrote, 'in refusing them any amenity which does not detract from the measures taken for their safe custody.' By lowering the security around the internees, Boland was not only attempting to make the job of guarding the men easier; he was also alive to any potential diplomatic problem which conditions inside the camp might cause. At this early stage in the war, only Germans had been detained, but Boland was looking to the future. As he put it:

> I am satisfied that this is not only the course dictated by the general practice of neutrals in the treatment of military internees, but that in our particular circumstance, it is the wisest policy to pursue. What we have to remember, I think, is that, before the war is over, we may have military internees of other than German nationality. The internment of members of the British Armed Forces here would give rise to questions in some ways more difficult than any we have had to face in connection with the present six men, and what we must be sure of is that we do not now withhold reasonable and usual amenities which it might be later deemed expedient to grant to military internees of another nationality to obviate, for example, attacks in the British press.[15]

DOI: 10.1057/9781137446039.0005

Boland was eager to ensure than any future British internees would not be guarded as tightly as the first Germans and removing the more onerous restrictions now would prevent complaints from London, further negative press coverage or accusations of favouritism from Germany. Following this intervention from Boland, a set of draft regulations was drawn up for dealing with belligerent internees. In line with his suggestions, they acknowledged that the security of the camp was paramount, but that all measures would be taken to 'relieve the monotony of their captivity'. Alcohol, radio and newspapers were now all permitted and any security precautions 'should be taken as unobtrusively as circumstances permit'.[16] However, things were slow to change and on 27 September, Walshe wrote to the secretary of the Department of Defence, pointing out that conditions in K-Lines were still 'unduly rigorous and unsympathetic'.[17]

The weight attached to the diplomatic dimensions of internment can be judged by the fact that, on 2 October 1940, the Department of External Affairs took the leading role in running K-Lines. While the Irish military remained in charge of the security surrounding the camp, all major decisions regarding the conditions inside the wire (including living conditions, parole and prevention of escapes) were from that point approved by External Affairs first, usually by Boland himself, and sometimes also had to receive de Valera's sanction. At a conference in February 1941, Boland reinforced the point that the conditions within the camp had implications for Ireland's relationship with the warring powers. Discussing the issue of parole for the internees, he said that

> in the view of the diplomatic representatives – and this is in accordance with the generally accepted international point of view – belligerent internees in a Neutral State are, to a certain extent, guests of the State and that it was desirable, therefore, that they should be granted all possible concessions consistent with the necessary precautions against their escape. (Irish Military Archives, S/231 'Conference at the Dept of Defence on the 1st February, 1941)

Interventions from diplomatic representatives also prompted Boland to alter the frequency with which internees could contact their Legations from quarterly to monthly. He further mentioned that Hempel had made several requests that Irish officers adopt a friendlier attitude towards the German internees, to which Colonel McNally replied that this created some difficulties, because of 'political opinions'.[18] He was either worried that his officers were pro-Allied or were pro-German and that either would complicate their interactions with the Germans, but this was not confirmed in the document.

DOI: 10.1057/9781137446039.0005

Once Allied aircrew began to arrive in the camp, the diplomatic scrutiny increased. The Canadian minister in Dublin supplied the B camp with a radio and the UK representative in Ireland, Sir John Maffey, was a frequent visitor. Over the course of three days in May 1941, the Polish Consul General, Maffey and two other British representatives visited the British internees.[19] From February 1942, an Air Ministry official was detailed to report directly to London every fortnight on conditions within the camp.[20] However, this also operated in reverse: when it became known that German internees were regularly travelling outside their parole area, Boland requested that the details of the violations be sent to the German minister.[21] Rather than the Irish authorities penalising the internees and possibly causing ill-will, Boland hoped that Hempel would put a stop to the practice. The men would still be punished, but there would be no danger of a diplomatic incident if Hempel handled the issue himself.

As de Valera occupied the External Affairs portfolio as well as being Taoiseach, representations from the belligerent diplomats all reached him directly or through either Walshe or Boland. Not all of the belligerents were so interested in their internees: Stephen Tanner has alleged that the US Legation in Switzerland did next to nothing to improve the conditions of US airmen in Swiss punishment camps,[22] while T. Ryle Dwyer suggested that the Canadian representative in Dublin was not eager to visit K-Lines[23] and that the Canadian government did not even know how many Canadians were held in the Curragh.[24] The Canadian minister appears infrequently on the visitor list in the Irish archives, while Maffey or his officials visited on a very regular basis. However, as it is unclear whether the Canadians in K-Lines were members of the Royal Air Force or the Canadian, the absence of the Canadian minister cannot be definitely be classified as disinterest.

From October 1940 onwards, many of the conferences in which parole and other conditions were set were either held in the offices of External Affairs or were attended by Boland. There are also several letters in the internment files contained in the Irish Military Archives from Joseph Walshe and de Valera himself attended a conference on parole conditions for internees in 1942. In addition to that, the living conditions of the internees were discussed at the Cabinet Committee on Emergency Problems, which dealt with issues arising from neutrality and the war and was attended by both ministers and high-ranking civil servants. As already mentioned, from October 1940, External Affairs had the final say

DOI: 10.1057/9781137446039.0005

on issues such as parole, which had initially been left at the discretion of the officer commanding of the Curragh; for example, in November 1941, the army Adjutant-General wrote to External Affairs, asking them to set time limits on internee parole,[25] which the PA would then enforce. The entry of the United States into the war in December l941 changed the dynamic of the Irish internment regime. Dublin had a strained relationship with America throughout 1940, and it deteriorated further in 1941 as Washington moved ever closer to the Allies. In public de Valera made attempts to reassure Roosevelt of his pro-Allied leanings. During a speech in Cork, a week after Pearl Harbour, de Valera declared that Ireland was pursuing a policy of 'friendly neutrality' towards the Allies.[26] To make matters worse, de Valera had a poor personal relationship with the US minister in Ireland, David Gray, which was a most unfortunate situation given that Gray was related to Roosevelt and had the President's ear. Gray was both a passionate believer in the Allied cause and an outspoken opponent of Irish neutrality. His actions in Dublin during the war have not endeared him to Irish historians: he has been described by Dermot Keogh as 'a troublemaker' who remained ignorant of the intricacies of Irish politics for the whole of his tenure as minister.[27] However, Gray's negative attitude towards neutrality, although sometimes inelegantly expressed, only mirrored that of Roosevelt and the administration. Washington did not approve of Dublin's stance during the war and steadfastly refused to provide any arms or military equipment to Eire while de Valera declined to cooperate overtly with Britain. A visit by Frank Aiken, the Irish Minister for the Coordination of Defensive Measures, to America in April 1941 had little chance of success and did not achieve very much. Indeed, the trip proved to be a complete disaster for Irish war-time diplomacy and Aiken, who was stubborn, dour and curt, was a poor choice of representative. His meeting with Roosevelt went legendarily badly: Aiken claimed that the President was so irritated during the interview that he knocked the cutlery from the table.[28] Aiken had hoped to secure American arms and funds for the Irish Defence Forces, but he returned with just two cargo ships and a promise of $500,000 in Red Cross Aid.[29]

Throughout 1941 there were persistent rumours that US personnel were preparing the port of Derry, in Northern Ireland, to be an American military base in the event of US involvement in the European war, and this added a further level of complication to Irish-US relations. The de Valera government maintained an irredentist claim to the territory of Northern

DOI: 10.1057/9781137446039.0005

Ireland, the six counties which had remained within the UK when the island was partitioned by the British government in 1922. Dublin's claim was enshrined in article two of the 1937 Constitution; the presence of American troops in Northern Ireland presented de Valera with a thorny problem. Because of the claim on the territory, de Valera felt he had to make a public statement on the US presence there, but anything that was too strongly worded risked further alienating Washington. When the first wave of American personnel finally arrived at the end of January 1942, de Valera compromised and issued what was effectively a non-protesting protest:[30] after stating that Ireland had no quarrel with the United States, it went on to say that it was the government's 'duty to make it clearly understood that no matter what troops occupy the Six Counties, the Irish people's claim for the union of the whole of the national territory and for supreme jurisdiction over it will remain unabated'.[31] This still publicly registered Dublin's interest in the territory, but was carefully calibrated not to antagonise Washington too much.

The arrival of US personnel in the North coincided with a huge increase in American flights in and around Ireland. Beginning in mid-1942, there was a mounting list of landings in Eire by American military aircraft, as Washington began to transfer vast quantities of men, machines and material to the UK. The Irish government approached this new situation with the same caution as it had the issue of US troops in Ulster. Throughout 1942–43, despite an ever-increasing number of landings and crashes by US aircraft, no American personnel were ever interned. Although no document has yet been found which tracks the origin of this decision, records exist of meetings between Joseph Walshe and David Gray in late 1942 and January 1943. Despite the fact that Walshe did not like Gray, the two men were able to put their personal feelings aside and come to an agreement regarding American flights in Ireland. At the first meeting, Gray asked the Irish government to draw a distinction between US aircraft which were on ferry or training flights, and those which were on combat flights; what Walshe suggested was that the two categories be referred to as 'non-operational' and 'operational'. Gray also unsubtly stated that should Ireland intern American aircrew, the US State Department would raise the matter after the war and that if Americans were detained in the Curragh, 'it would be impossible to keep this news from American correspondents'. He further requested that Dublin regard all German overflights as being operational and, therefore, subject to internment if they landed.[32]

DOI: 10.1057/9781137446039.0005

Walshe replied that Ireland's attitude was one of 'friendly neutrality' – deliberately repeating de Valera's words of December 1941 – and he dropped the equally unsubtle hint that Dublin intended interning belligerent aircrew on operational flights only. He also requested that any agreement be kept unofficial, as committing something to paper would be likely to 'create difficulties'.[33] US Secretary of State Cordell Hull agreed with this, as he felt that the agreement contravened international precedents that had been set during the First World War.[34] However, in order to avoid having to intern any Americans, Walshe explicitly warned Gray to remind all US aircrew to claim they were on non-operational flights if they were detained by Irish security forces after landing in Eire. Walshe further pointed out that after one such crash-landing, Irish officers had to actually create a cover story for an American pilot in order to be able to release him.[35] This was a major issue for the Irish authorities before the Walshe-Gray meetings: the crew of five of the first six US aircraft which landed in Ireland after Washington entered the war did not claim to be on non-operational flights but were released anyway.[36] In January 1944, a document found near a crashed US aircraft in county Kilkenny proved that Gray had heeded Walshe's advice: the paper instructed American aircrew that, if they landed in Ireland, they were to emphasise '"WE ARE ON A NON-OPERATION FLIGHT" NOTHING ELSE'.[37] It was further agreed that an American officer would be detailed to act as a liaison between Dublin, Washington and the forces in Northern Ireland when US aircraft landed.[38]

The guidelines suggested by Gray became Irish policy. In February 1943, Michael Rynne sketched out the evolving Irish approach, stating that, as the sheer number of belligerent aircraft in operation made the Hague rules impossible to enforce, each neutral was forced to do 'what it can within the framework of its special difficulties to build up a body of rules or customs based on the broad principles of international law'.[39] In a long memorandum in April 1944, he set out what had now become the government's official stance. The 'essential criteria on which the Government's internment policy depends' wrote Rynne, were

> (a) Airmen are interned when they land on Irish territory during operational flights, (b) they are released when they are land during non-operational flights, (c) Allied airmen are presumed to be on non-operational flights unless the contrary is proved by us and (d) German airmen are presumed to be on an operational flight unless the contrary is proved by them.[40]

DOI: 10.1057/9781137446039.0005

This formula, combined with the fact that by 1942 Eire had disregarded international law as a framework for belligerent internment and instead relied on Irish legislation, allowed Dublin to operate what was effectively three separate internment regimes: US aircrew were never interned, regardless of the circumstances of their arrival in Ireland. British and Commonwealth personnel were almost always released, except when they had transparently been on a combat mission, while German personnel were consistently detained, no matter what their status. The fact that all Americans went free while British pilots were still subject to occasional internment was, as Rynne noted, an 'absurd state of affairs' which 'actually discriminates between Allies, both equally entitled to the full benefit of the presumption in their favour'.[41]

The result was that during 1942, despite 35 Allied planes coming down on Irish soil, only one pilot was interned.[42] On at least one occasion, an Allied aircraft was classified as being on a non-combat flight, even when the Irish authorities believed otherwise. In April 1942, an RAF Curtis Tomahawk landed in Wicklow. The pilot stated that he was on a training flight from Scotland; however, Dan Bryan of G2 suspected 'that he was in pursuit of a German aircraft which had preceded him southwards along the coastline'.[43] The pilot was briefly interned, then released.[44] From 1943 to the end of the war, a further 77 Allied aircraft landed in Ireland, with only five crew being interned.[45] When Hempel attempted to have a German aircraft which crashed in Tipperary during December 1943 classed as non-operational, Walshe refused, arguing that the crew had destroyed the craft and the ensuing explosion was heard 'fifty miles away'; he 'could not imagine a training plane having so much explosives aboard'. He further explained to Hempel that Dublin could not regard any German aircraft landing in Ireland as being non-operational, on the reasonable grounds that British aerodromes were extremely close to Ireland, whereas German planes had to fly hundreds of miles to enter Irish airspace.[46] Hempel was unable to challenge this argument and his inability to move Walshe from this position showed the weak diplomatic hand Germany had to play at this stage of the war.

This policy caused de Valera some awkward moments in the Dáil and independent TD Oliver Flanagan was particularly determined to pin de Valera down on the anomalous operation of the internment policy. When asked in November 1943 about belligerent aircraft being allowed to leave, the Taoiseach replied tersely that 'Those which were engaged on operational flights were detained and their crews interned. The others were released'.[47] When questioned again in February 1944 by Flanagan, de Valera referred him back to his November 1943 answer, and refused to provide any more details.[48] Flanagan persisted, and asked that if British pilots were being released, why were Germans still being detained, 'if we are neutral?'[49] De Valera declined to answer yet another question on the subject from the determined Flanagan on 28 June 1944.[50]

The Irish policy led to some celebrated incidents that were widely known to the public despite the wish of the Irish government to keep them confidential. In January 1943 a USAF B-17 crashed in a field in Athenry, county Galway, in the west of Ireland. The aircraft was carrying several high-ranking officers on board, including US General Jacob Devers and Lt. General Edward Brooks. Local legend states that the Americans thought they had landed in enemy territory, as an Irish-speaking battalion of the Local Defence Force (LDF) arrived to secure the site and the US aircrew could not understand the language. Devers spoke freely with Irish military officers about the war situation, conditions in liberated areas and the training in the US army, information which was carefully recorded by G2 and which was passed onto de Valera himself.[51] In the meantime, they were entertained in a local hotel and handed out souvenirs to visitors. The aircraft crashed at around midday on 15 January and by 2 AM the next morning, the crew and all of the eminent passengers had been ferried to the border with Northern Ireland,[52] crossing over at Belleek. Another B-17 which flew over Dublin in April 1943 was made to feel less welcome, when Irish anti-aircraft guns opened fire on it, forcing it to land at Dublin airport, whereupon it was refuelled and released. The incident led to instructions being issued to gunners that Allied aircraft were not to be fired upon unless they were transparently hostile. This mirrored orders given to Swedish anti-aircraft defences to fire only warning shots at German and Finnish aircraft in Swedish airspace during the early phase of the Axis invasion of the USSR in June 1941.[53] Shortly afterwards the incident at Dublin airport, de Valera himself explicitly reminded US officials that the current Irish policy was not rooted in any international regulations and that it was operating exclusively in favour of the Allies.[54] In yet another example, an American C-47 carrying armed US officers landed at Rineanna airport, where it remained overnight; both Defence and External Affairs were consulted before it was released to fly to Northern Ireland.[55]

Dublin attempted to keep track of the internment policy of other European neutrals, particularly once the change in policy had been

DOI: 10.1057/9781137446039.0005

decided upon, in order to reassure itself that it was not committing a major breach of neutrality by releasing Allied aircraft and crews. The major difficulty was in actually getting information from the continent in the midst of the war and early in the conflict Boland lamented that Ireland could not obtain details of how other neutrals were dealing with the issue.[56] Moreover, when the information arrived, it was debateable whether it could actually be relied upon. The Irish Legation in Berlin sent news in October 1943 that Switzerland had begun to release equal numbers of Allied and German personnel. Documents from the Swedish Consul-General informed Dublin that Sweden interned all belligerent personnel arriving on its territory, but External Affairs suspected that 'at least prior to May 1943, German military aircraft were allowed to take off with all their crew as soon necessary repairs had been effected'. External Affairs also gleaned from the *Daily Express* that British crews were now being released after landing in Sweden. Details of internment in Turkey and Portugal were sketchy, but the best information available to de Valera was that both seemed to have released their belligerent internees.[57] The government tried to stay in touch with developments in Sweden through the *Swedish News* pamphlet, which remain in the Irish National Archives, but which rarely mentioned military internees.[58] In reality, all European neutrals, excluding Switzerland, adjusted their internment regimes as the course of the war dictated. Sweden, under pressure from Germany, initially followed a strict policy of interning all Allied personnel while offering concessions to the Luftwaffe, similar to those given by Ireland to the RAF and Coastal Command. Eventually 1218 US aircrew were held in Sweden.[59] During the war, German medical and courier flights were allowed to overfly Swedish airspace.[60] From 1944, it began large-scale releases of Allied internees in return for US bombers and fighter aircraft.[61] During 1944, the Swedes released 935 British and Americans, 121 Russians, 20 Poles and 328 Germans.[62] Although a post-war investigation found that Spain offered extensive assistance to German intelligence, aircraft and submarines,[63] Franco also usually allowed US airmen to transit through Spain to Gibraltar rather than intern them.[64] Portugal temporarily interned both Allied and German personnel[65] as did Turkey.[66] The Swiss government authorised an exchange agreement with both the Allies and the Germans in February 1945, a process which was complicated by the fact that the number of Allied escapes from Swiss camps meant there was some difficulty in arriving at an accurate figure for Allied internees.[67] However, Swiss policy was close to Ireland's in one

DOI: 10.1057/9781137446039.0005

respect: Switzerland occasionally released pilots who had become lost over the country on the grounds that, if they had not been on a combat mission, the Hague obligation to intern did not apply.[68] Rynne explicitly placed Ireland and Switzerland in the same category when dealing with belligerent overflights.[69]

It is clear that Irish policy on internment and releases was extremely close to other European neutrals, which also disregarded international law when they could. Sweden, Turkey and Spain all purchased salvaged Allied aircraft after crash-landing; likewise, during the course of the war, Dublin bought one Hudson bomber, three Hurricane fighters, one Fairey Battle and one Miles Master training aircraft, all of which were recovered after crashing or force-landing.[70] Another parallel was the destruction or removal of secret aircraft equipment. In April 1943, Maffey asked that all British aircrews be allowed to remove any 'secret equipment' in the event of a crash-landing, to which Oscar Traynor, Minister for Defence, agreed.[71] Similarly, the Swiss on one occasion agreed to destroy a specially modified and secret model of German ME-110 nightfighter which landed near Zurich in 1944. Unlike the Irish, however, the Swiss extracted a high price: in return, they received 12 ME-109 fighter aircraft.[72]

The frequency with which Allied aircraft and crew were being released eventually sparked written protests from the German Minister in Dublin. On 21 May 1943, he wrote a letter detailing six releases which he knew of; on 27 July he wrote again, asking that an equal number of Germans be released.[73] At a meeting with Walshe on 15 September 1943, Hempel complained that 'nothing could be more serious than the act of allowing planes to depart from our custody in order to fight against the German Armed Forces and to drop bombs on civilians'. In reply, Walshe replied that Ireland had decided to adopt the 'non-operational' principle and that all releases of Allied aircraft came within this definition.[74] On 30 November, the disconcertingly well-informed Hempel sent an official note of protest against the Irish policy, pointing out that at least one of the Allied pilots released by the Irish government had re-entered active military service against Germany. However, a meeting between Hempel and Walshe at the end of November illustrated the dwindling German ability to pressure Ireland. When Hempel later stated that Berlin did not recognise the distinction drawn between operational and non-operational flights, and requested the release of German personnel on the basis of reciprocity, Walshe told him bluntly that he 'did not hold out any hope that his men could be released'.[75]

DOI: 10.1057/9781137446039.0005

The contrast between the inability of Germany to make any impression on the internment regime and the ever-growing influence of the Allies over it became increasingly marked throughout 1943 and 1944. At the same time as Hempel was protesting to Walshe, Dublin was also coming under sustained pressure from London, particularly concerning the inconsistent Irish approach toward American, British and Commonwealth personnel. Maffey had previously attempted to extract compromises from the Irish government: in July 1942, Walshe complained to Peadar MacMahon at Defence that every time internment was discussed with Maffey, 'it gives an opportunity for a request for concessions, the extent and impossibility of which you can well imagine'.[76] From 1943 onwards, the UK representative in Dublin launched a much more persistent campaign to further tilt the Irish interment regime towards the Allies, which de Valera had difficulty in resisting as he had already sanctioned concessions towards the Americans. In February 1943, Maffey warned de Valera that after the war London would have difficulty forgetting that Eire detained British airmen and allowed Axis Legations to remain open.[77] In May, seeking the release of the RAF personnel in K-Lines, Maffey dropped heavy hints about the 'common supply line' that Ireland and the UK shared across the Atlantic, as well as the 'unhappiness and resentment which have spread from that camp to English homes and throughout the Commonwealth, casting long shadows'. At the same time, he argued the internment policy actually cost Allied lives, as damaged aircraft had crashed while trying to avoid landing in Ireland.[78] In July he pressed home his attack on the spot where de Valera was weakest:

> the detention of RAF will put the Eire Government in a position of grave embarrassment when an American crew is force-landed here from operations. This will certainly happen and may happen at any moment. I should be surprised to hear that the Eire Government have any intention of enforcing internment in such a case. The clash that would then occur between the Eire Government and the British Government in regard to the RAF internees is obvious.[79]

Under severe pressure from London, de Valera finally agreed to release Allied internees who were deemed not to have been on operational flights when they had landed in Ireland. Accordingly, twenty men were released in October 1943, and the others moved to a new camp near Gormanstown. Maffey informed the Dominions Office that this

DOI: 10.1057/9781137446039.0005

development meant that British aircraft could operate around Eire 'on the assumption that no risk of internment exists'.[80] He also renewed his campaign for the release of the remaining eleven internees, while seeking assurances that the Irish government would not try to release any Germans. In a meeting with Walshe on 11 October, Maffey stressed that the remaining internees were a 'running sore' in Anglo-Irish relations and London would 'find it very hard to reconcile the continued internment of British airmen while we refrained from interning American airmen'.[81]

Such constant pressing by Maffey inevitably caused some irritation within the Irish government, particularly from Frederick Boland, who was primarily responsible for the belligerent internees in the Curragh. Writing on 13 October 1943, Boland argued for a rebalancing of the internment policy. He felt that it would make much more sense if *all* the internees, Axis as well as Allied, could be released. His preference was for an agreement with the UK under which all would be set free, in return for a promise not to intern any more Allied personnel who landed in Ireland. In Boland's view, this would 'involve far less political and other risks than the continuance of our current policy of granting every possible latitude to one side – to the point of interning only 6 of the 200 odd Allied airmen who landed here in the last 21 months – while visiting the utmost rigour of the law on the other'.[82] Michael Rynne also noted irritably in 1944 that Britain seemed to expect far more of Eire than other European neutrals.[83]

Diplomatic considerations undoubtedly also played the central role in de Valera's decision to intern 164 German sailors, who arrived in Cobh on 1 January 1944. The Germans had been rescued by the Irish coaster *Kerlogue*, after the destroyer *Z27* and torpedo boats *T25* and *T26* had been sunk by the Royal Navy in the Bay of Biscay. The survivors estimated that only thirty per cent of those who had been forced to abandon their ships were eventually found.[84] The *Kerlogue* refused to follow British instructions to put into a British port, as the captain argued that the sailors required medical attention, and he was proved correct as four of them died after their rescue.[85] Once they landed, the sailors were questioned by G2, and this information was later passed to the Office of Strategic Services (OSS), the American intelligence agency.[86] The arrival of the sailors presented a severe problem for de Valera. It was clear that the government had little idea what would happen once the *Kerlogue* found survivors, or that they would even reach Ireland, as they might be forced

DOI: 10.1057/9781137446039.0005

to deliver them to the British. Walshe informed Hempel that although the men would be rescued, 'we could give no guarantee whatever as to what would happen to the men when they had been picked up', as Irish ships were subject to British contraband control.[87] Under the terms of the 1907 Convention, those rescued could be classed as distressed mariners; if the government chose this path, the men were exempt from internment. However, the Government was advised as early as September 1939 that the actual regulations regarding shipwrecked sailors were not comprehensive, and that 'neutrals are free to do what they like in the matter'.[88] As previously noted, Michael Rynne had already in June 1940 recommended the internment of sailors of all nationalities who came ashore in Ireland following the fall of France.

Moreover, the British government could not countenance such a large body of Germans being set free within Eire where they could potentially make contact with the IRA or gather intelligence on Allied forces in Northern Ireland, particularly with the landings at Normandy only a few months away. As under-secretary for Dominion Affairs, Paul Emrys-Evans said in the House of Commons on 20 January 1944, London had ensured that Dublin was 'fully alive to the importance of keeping these men properly interned'.[89] The Department of Defence had already highlighted its unease about the possibility of German agents, posing as shipwrecked sailors, making contact with the IRA. Releasing them in Ireland, Defence argued, 'would offer an ideal way for disaffected elements to secure the services of skilled technicians to carry on work detrimental to the security of the State'.[90] Even without British pressure and regardless of international convention, Dublin was inclined to intern the survivors in any case.

Maffey argued that concessions to Germany, which would see *any* Germans released from interment, would 'impair the Taoiseach's pledge not to allow this country to be used as a base against us'. As might be expected, he approved of de Valera's action in interning the sailors, and used that precedent to argue against any leeway being offered to Germany.[91] In fact, when Walshe informed Norman Archer of the Dominions Office that the *Kerlogue* was seeking German survivors, Archer callously suggested that, since the location of the sailors was uncertain, Dublin might order the ships not to turn back and search for them.[92] However, the decision to detain the sailors was eventually made before they had landed: when Maffey contacted Walshe in the early hours of 1 January and requested that Dublin intern them, Walshe

DOI: 10.1057/9781137446039.0005

informed him that 'he was certain that this was the intention of the Taoiseach'.[93] This was in direct contrast to the orders given by Frederick Boland in November 1941, who pointed out to the Department of Justice that Allied convoy ships often carried Royal Navy gun crews and, if these men washed ashore in Ireland following a shipwreck, would be liable to internment if they were still in uniform. He asked that Justice instruct Gardaí encountering these men to ensure that they changed into civilian uniform while they were travelling through Eire.[94] Likewise, in June 1944 the Defence Forces issued instructions that all naval craft and crew which came ashore in Ireland were to be taken into military custody and to wait for further orders; because there was no actual mention of internment, David Gray felt that this was an indication that de Valera wanted to secretly release all Allied naval crew who washed ashore in Eire.[95] When measured against these, the decision to intern the German sailors can be seen to have been rooted overwhelmingly in diplomatic considerations, primarily the desire not to further antagonise Britain, combined with the fear of the IRA recruiting the sailors. However, given that at this stage of the war the IRA was disintegrating, the diplomatic explanation is the more likely one.

This is even more obvious when placed in the context of the arrangement between Dublin and London regarding the landing of British sailors who were brought ashore at Moville, a coastal town in county Donegal. In September 1941, the British government requested that crew who were injured or ill while on British vessels in Lough Foyle be allowed to land at Moville and be ferried to Derry by ambulance, which was only a few miles away by road. Once the British had assured Dublin that the sailors would be in civilian clothes, de Valera himself gave his permission for the arrangement to proceed.[96] The plan required the involvement of several government departments: the Department of Defence had to be notified about the possibility of British service personnel landing in Donegal, the Department of Justice had to instruct the Gardaí to allow the ambulances to cross the border into Northern Ireland, and the Revenue Commissioners had to be informed, as they controlled the customs posts along the border. The Gardaí were also instructed to observe and report on the operation of the arrangement.[97] The parallel is far from direct: transporting injured British sailors a few miles to hospital across neutral territory is very different from releasing over 160 German sailors to live in neutral Ireland for the duration of the

DOI: 10.1057/9781137446039.0005

war. However, it still illustrates yet another aspect of Irish cooperation with the Allies which was denied to Germany, and it is very difficult to imagine de Valera agreeing so readily to a similar arrangement with Berlin.

As Michael Rynne observed in April 1944, detaining the German sailors only opened the door to further pressure from London. When Maffey urged de Valera to arrest and hold all Germans who landed in Ireland, Rynne noted that Maffey based this argument on 'our departure from normal international practice in the case of the German naval ratings who were rescued by an Irish merchantman but, nevertheless, interned'.[98] Having moved so far to meet Allied requests, de Valera had little scope to refuse them when they came looking for more.

Oliver Flanagan's questions to de Valera in the Dáil regarding releases sparked another missive from Maffey in February 1944, again asking that the remaining Allied internees should be considered to have been on non-operational flights and therefore released. He referred to Dublin's move away from international law in interning the German sailors, and again hinted at the preference offered to US aircrew: 'I need not drag in', he wrote, 'the practice in the case of America, nor stress the anomalies to which it has led'.[99] This was followed by yet another letter in April 1944, claiming that the 'spirit and morale' of the Allied internees, since October 1943 re-located to Gormanstown, was suffering. Significantly, Maffey also mentioned that the British Dominions Secretary, Viscount Cranborne, had also taken an interest in the case. He clearly had realised that he alone did not carry sufficient weight to push de Valera into a decision, and the mention of Cranborne was designed to further pressurise the government.[100]

Because of the extensive concessions already offered by de Valera, his ability to refuse Maffey's request was limited. Neutrality had been originally based, Rynne argued, on international law combined with de Valera's pledge not to allow Eire to be used as a base to attack the UK. However, as the war went on, it became harder and harder to reconcile these two and Dublin tended to lean towards fulfilling the latter rather than rigidly adhering to international regulations. The internment regime as it evolved towards a firmly pro-Allied position had tended to reinforce the Taoiseach's pledge, at the cost of international law. As Rynne stated, by 1944 Ireland had been forced by British pressure to leave international law 'far behind'. He also recognised that the situation was largely of Ireland's own making, as he advised the government to

DOI: 10.1057/9781137446039.0005

face the fact that since the first American plane landed in Ireland (July 1942) not a single US machine has been interned (28 landed or crashed) and the fact that since that date more than half of the forty or so British planes which landed were assisted to leave at once. In many of these cases appearances were altogether against the planes concerned but the presumption "non-operational" won out; sometimes the issue was decided by the mere word of the interested belligerent.[101]

In other words, the government's policy of offering extreme leniency towards the Allies, rather than placating them, actually led to demands for even more. Rynne's observation that Dublin sometimes relied on the assurances of the Allies also directly contradicted Walshe's statement to Hempel in December 1943, in which he explicitly told the German minister that Ireland 'never accepted the word of the British or Americans as to the character, operational or otherwise, of a plane. We always had to examine the plane and see for ourselves'.[102]

De Valera attempted to resist Maffey's request to release the remaining internees, saying in early June that Dublin had gone as far as it could. However, during a meeting between the two, Maffey effectively issued the Taoiseach an ultimatum: he was travelling to London where he would deliver the news of de Valera's failure to cooperate on the issue.[103] Maffey was suggesting that he would report Dublin's refusal to the British cabinet, transferring responsibility out of Maffey's hands to higher authorities. Potentially faced with another diplomatic incident following on so close from the so-called American Note in February 1944, de Valera agreed to the British request. On 13 June Maffey was informed that, 'in view of the personal representations of Lord Cranborne... and as a friendly gesture', de Valera had decided to release the rest of the Allied internees. Along with the official typed memo recording this was an anonymous handwritten note, which stated that the 'concession made on representation', presumably meaning that it was the actual intervention by Cranborne personally that had finally persuaded de Valera to act. Although this was not stated in the documents, fear of further economic restrictions on Ireland, and the success of the Allied landings at Normandy, which meant the end of the war had come into sight, probably also played a role in his decision.

The departure of the Allied internees effectively removed the diplomatic dimension of internment. The Germans' lives increasingly revolved around domestic issues: the move to the new camp in 1944, the settling-in process of the sailors, the declining morale amongst the

DOI: 10.1057/9781137446039.0005

internees and, as Germany crumbled, the need to find employment as funds from Berlin dried up.

No mention has yet been made in this chapter of Dublin's attitude towards prisoners of war held abroad. This is because, from a diplomatic point of view, there was nothing that the government could do for them. Even had he wished to intervene, de Valera did not have the legal standing, the diplomatic clout or up-to-date information from prisoner of war camps to allow Dublin to act. When asked by concerned citizens to officially protest to Japan against the treatment of Allied prisoners in their hands, the government issued no response. External Affairs relied on newspaper clippings from the Irish Legation in Washington to keep abreast of events in the Far East, which were forwarded by the Irish minister there, Robert Brennan, detailing the depth of American public anger against the Japanese.[104] Similarly, in June 1941, the Irish representative in Italy, Michael MacWhite, informed External Affairs that a priest had been sent to minister to Irish prisoners of war in Germany. External Affairs recommended that Dublin not get involved:

> ... there could be no objection to Irish priest going from Rome to look after spiritual needs of Irish prisoners if the latter want him. You should leave the matter to the Church authorities. It is their affair. Any intervention by you makes it political... Also danger of our attitude of strict neutrality being misunderstood.[105]

It transpired that the priest had visited prisoner of war camps in which Irish were held separately and where the Germans were attempting to recruit prisoners for anti-British activities. Upon learning this, G2 became intensely interested, but there remained little that Dublin could do except ask for further reports from MacWhite. Concerns over the international reaction also led the government to – with genuine reluctance – turn down an International Red Cross request to take in injured prisoners of war to convalesce in Ireland. Neither the Irish military nor the Department of Local Government and Public Health had available hospital space to turn over to prisoners, but Rynne also remarked that 'the British might have political objections to allowing Axis prisoners to roam at large in Ireland'.[106] Given London's reaction to the arrival of the German sailors in 1944, this was an accurate observation. But, as Brendan O'Riordan observed, Germany was equally likely to object to the plan, as Ireland's proximity to the UK meant that some of the prisoners

DOI: 10.1057/9781137446039.0005

would try to escape back to their units and rejoin the war.[107] Frederick Boland also had one eye on Ireland's reputation amongst other European neutrals when discussing the issue. As he put it, Ireland was 'one of the last few remaining neutral states to make some effort to co-operate'. If Dublin had to refuse, Boland wanted 'some convincing explanation of the reasons why we find ourselves unable to do so'.[108]

Conclusion

In October 1942, Maffey wrote to Walshe regarding the Allied internees in K-Lines, reminding him that it was a serious Anglo-Irish issue.

> The fact is that the handling of all matters relating to these internees is to-day far more important from an external than from an internal point of view. Owing to the force of circumstances to-day no Department of the Eire Government – and I include the Defence Department – can regard with indifference the imperilling of friendly relations with the Departments of the Allied Nations.[109]

Maffey's warning was not required in Dublin. Throughout the war, the Irish government consistently prioritised the diplomatic aspects of belligerent internment. When it came to choosing between the application of international law or maintaining the Irish-Allied relationship, the de Valera government invariably chose the latter, to the extent that the Irish internment system functioned in favour of the Allies. Concessions made to America from 1942 onwards inevitably led to the same concessions being made for the UK. Ireland was not alone in choosing this path; with the exception of Switzerland, other European neutrals, even Franco's Spain, altered their military internment systems in order to favour the Allies, usually after the US entered the war. Diplomacy became a major consideration in Ireland's belligerent internment policy largely because there were neither precise rules laid out for the detention of belligerent personnel, nor any consensus among neutrals how to interpret international law. The signing of the 1949 Geneva Convention, theoretically at least, removed the need to take international relations into consideration but, as Ireland has never again been called upon to detain international military personnel, this is a theory that remains untested.

DOI: 10.1057/9781137446039.0005

Notes

1   The National Archives, DO 114/117, WX 101/92, 'Neutrality of Eire (World War 1939–1945) Correspondence and Papers', note from Archer to Stephenson, 11 April 1945.

2   Fisk, *In Time of War*, p. 327.

3   Ibid., p. 176.

4   D. Ferriter (2007) *Judging Dev: A Reassessment of the Life and Legacy of Eamon de Valera* (Dublin: Royal Irish Academy), p. 256.

5   National Archives of Ireland, DFA A/26, 'Summary of chronological list of forced landings, or crashes of Belligerent aircraft from the outbreak of war to 30.6.45', undated list.

6   Dáil debates, 29 January 1935.

7   *Documents on Irish Foreign Policy, Volume V*, p. 495.

8   *Documents on Irish Foreign Policy Volume VI*, p. 17.

9   Ibid., p. 23.

10 D. MacCarron (2003) *Landfall Ireland: The Story of Allied and German Aircraft Which Came down in Éire in World War Two* (Newtownards: Colourpoint Books), p. 15.

11 M. Kennedy (2008) *Guarding Neutral Ireland: The Coast Watching Service and Military Intelligence* (Dublin: Four Courts Press), p. 138.

12 Kennedy, *Guarding Neutral Ireland*, p. 37.

13 Irish Military Archives, PM336, Lennon to Arbour Hill, 25 September 1939.

14 Irish Military Archives, S/231, Boland to Archer, 5 September 1940.

15 Irish Military Archives, S/231, Boland to Archer, 5 September 1940.

16 Irish Military Archives, S/231, undated list of regulations.

17 Irish Military Archives, C229A, Walshe to MacMahon, 27 September 1940.

18 Irish Military Archives, S/231 'Conference at the Department of Defence on the 1st February, 1941'.

19 Irish Military Archives, PM 733P, list of visitors.

20 National Archives of Ireland, DFA A/44, 'Escape of British Internees Parole arrangements, etc', report by Walshe, 24 February 1942.

21 Irish Military Archives, C229, notes of meeting 10 January 1944.

22 Tanner, *Refuge from the Reich*, p. 195.

23 Dwyer, *Guests of the State*, p. 101.

24 Ibid., p. 128.

25 Irish Military Archives, C229A, O'hAodh to Cashman, 4 December 1941.

26 J.P. O'Carroll, and J.A. Murphy, (1983) *De Valera and His Times* (Cork: Cork University Press), p. 117.

27 D. Keogh (2005) *Twentieth-Century Ireland: Revolution and State Building* (Dublin: Gill & Macmillan), p. 120.

28 Fisk, *In Time of War*, p. 308.

DOI: 10.1057/9781137446039.0005

29 J.L. Rosenberg (1980) 'The 1941 Mission of Frank Aiken to the United States: An American Perspective' *Irish Historical Studies*, 22, 86, 168.

30 T.P. Coogan (1993) *De Valera: Long Fellow, Long Shadow* (London: Hutchinson), p. 594.

31 Coogan, *De Valera*, p. 594.

32 National Archives of Ireland, DFA A/26, Gray to Walshe, 22 December 1942.

33 National Archives of Ireland, DFA A/26, Walshe to Gray, 11 December 1942.

34 Meares, 'Neutral States and the Application of International Law', 89.

35 Kennedy, *Guarding Neutral Ireland*, p. 217.

36 Dwyer, *Behind the Green Curtain*, p. 247.

37 National Archives of Ireland, DFA A/26, 'Forced landing in Neutral Territory', undated. Underline and capitals in the original.

38 National Archives of Ireland, DFA A/26, Gray to Walshe, 22 December 1942.

39 National Archives of Ireland, DFA A/26, 'Internment of Belligerent aircraft and airmen', memo by Rynne, 18 February 1943.

40 National Archives of Ireland, DFA A/50, memo by Rynne 11 April 1944.

41 National Archives of Ireland, DFA A/50, memo by Rynne, 11 April 1944.

42 Dwyer, *Guests of the State*, p. 114.

43 National Archives of Ireland, DFA A/26, memo by Bryan, 24 April 1942.

44 MacCarron, *Landfall Ireland*, p.117–18.

45 Dwyer, *Guests of the State*, p. 117.

46 National Archives of Ireland, DFA A/26, 'Release of German planes', 15 December 1943.

47 Dáil debates, 4 November 1943.

48 Dáil debates, 16 February 1944.

49 National Archives of Ireland, DFA A/26, Extract from Official Report of Dáil debates, 16 February 1944.

50 Dáil debates, 28 June 1944.

51 National Archives of Ireland, DFA A/26, Walshe to O'Connell, 13 July 1943.

52 P. Browne (2003) *Eagles over Ireland* (Athenry: Flying Fortress Athenry 1943), p. 39.

53 C.G. Scott (2002) 'The Swedish Midsummer crisis of 1941: The Crisis That Never War' *Journal of Contemporary History*, 37, 3, 378.

54 Kennedy, *Guarding Neutral Ireland*, p. 239.

55 National Archives of Ireland, DFA A/26, 'Landing of troop-carrying aircraft at Ryeana on 6/7/1942'.

56 Irish Military Archives, S/231, Boland to Archer, 5 September 1940.

57 National Archives of Ireland, DFA A/26, undated list.

58 National Archives of Ireland, DFA 233/107 and 233/107A.

59 Meares, 'Neutral States and the application of international' law', 87.

60 G. Ueberschär 'Strategy and Policy in Northern Europe' in H. Boog, J. Förster, J. Hoffman, E. Klink, R.D. Müller, G.R.Ueberschär (eds.) (1996) *Germany and the Second World War Volume IV: The Attack on the Soviet Union* (Oxford: Clarendon Press), p. 995.

DOI: 10.1057/9781137446039.0005

61   Meares, 'Neutral States and the application of international law', p. 88.
62   J. Gilmour (2010) *Sweden, the Swastika and Stalin: The Swedish Experience in the Second World War* (Edinburgh: Edinburgh University Press), p. 204.
63   P. Preston (1994) *Franco* (New York: Basic Books), p. 361.
64   Meares, 'Neutral States and the application of international law', p. 90.
65   Ibid., 94.
66   Ibid., 98.
67   Tanner, *Refuge from the Reich*, p. 205.
68   N. Wyllie (2003) *Britain, Switzerland and the Second World War* (Oxford: Oxford University Press), p. 317.
69   National Archives of Ireland, DFA A/26, 'Internment of Belligerent aircraft and airmen' memo by Rynne, 18 February 1943.
70   National Archives of Ireland, DFA A/26, 'Summary of chronological list of forced landings, or crashes of Belligerent aircraft from the outbreak of war to 30.6.45', undated list.
71   National Archives of Ireland, DFA A/26, Walshe to Maffey, 15 April 1943.
72   Tanner, *Refuge from the Reich*, p. 117.
73   National Archives of Ireland, DFA A/26, letters from Hempel.
74   National Archives of Ireland, DFA A/26, meeting between Walshe and Hempel, 15 September 1943.
75   National Archives of Ireland, DFA A/26, meeting between Walshe and Hempel, 15 December 1943.
76   National Archives of Ireland, DFA A/44, Walshe to MacMahon, 14 July, 1942.
77   D. Keogh and M. O' Driscoll (2004) *Ireland in World War Two: Neutrality and Survival* (Cork: Mercier Press), p. 120.
78   National Archives of Ireland, DFA A/50, letter from Maffey, May 1943.
79   National Archives of Ireland, DFA A/50, letter from Maffey, 30 July 1943.
80   Keogh and O' Driscoll, *Ireland in World War Two*, p. 120.
81   National Archives of Ireland, DFA A/50, memo by Walshe, 14 October 1943.
82   National Archives of Ireland, DFA A/50, memo by Boland, 13 October 1943.
83   National Archives of Ireland, DFA A/50, memo by Rynne, 11 April 1944.
84   National Archives of Ireland, DFA P80, 'Correspondence of German Naval Internees', undated.
85   M. Kennedy and V. Laing (2011) *The Irish Defence Forces 1940–1949: The Chiefs of Staff's Reports* (Dublin: Irish Manuscript Commission), p. 324.
86   Dwyer, *Behind the Green Curtain*, p. 308.
87   National Archives of Ireland, DFA P80', memo by Walshe, 5 January 1944.
88   Irish Military Archives, S/231 'Re Extension of 'Shipwrecked Sailor' doctrine to crews of military aircraft forced to land', 14 September 1939. Memo is unsigned but was presumably written by either Hayes or Rynne.
89   House of Commons debates, 19 January 1944, col 396, cc 385–86.
90   Irish Military Archives, S/231, undated Defence memo.

DOI: 10.1057/9781137446039.0005

91   National Archives of Ireland, DFA A/50, letter from Maffey, 18 February 1944.
92   National Archives of Ireland, DFA P80, memo by Walshe, 5 January 1944.
93   National Archives of Ireland, DFA P80, memo by Walshe, 7 January 1944.
94   National Archives of Ireland, JUS 90/119/316, Boland to Duff, 10 November 1941.
95   Kennedy, *Guarding Neutral Ireland*, p. 272.
96   National Archives of Ireland, DFA A/33, Boland to Defence, 18 September 1941.
97   National Archives of Ireland, DFA A/33, Boland to Justice, 29 September 1941.
98   National Archives of Ireland, DFA A/50, memo by Rynne, 11 April 1944.
99   National Archives of Ireland, DFA A/50, letter from Maffey, 18 February 1944.
100   National Archives of Ireland, DFA A/50, letter from Maffey, 29 April 1944.
101   National Archives of Ireland, DFA A/50, memo by Rynne, 11 April 1944.
102   National Archives of Ireland, DFA A/26, Walshe to de Valera, 15 December 1943.
103   Keogh and O' Driscoll, *Ireland in World War Two*, p. 123.
104   National Archives of Ireland, DFA 241/402, forwards from Brennan, 11 February 1944.
105   National Archives of Ireland, DFA A/36, telegram from External Affairs, 7 June 1941.
106   National Archives of Ireland, DFA 243/1038, memo by Rynne, 30 September 1943.
107   National Archives of Ireland, DFA 243/1038, memo by O'Riordan, 1 October 1943.
108   National Archives of Ireland, DFA 243/1038, memo by Boland, 13 October 1943.
109   National Archives of Ireland, DFA A/44, Maffey to Walshe, 21 October 1942.

DOI: 10.1057/9781137446039.0005

3
Settling in and Earning Their Keep: Life in K-Lines

Abstract: *K-Lines, the first of the belligerent internment camps in neutral Ireland, has consistently been misrepresented as a prisoner of war camp, and consequently the extensive concessions offered to the internees have been depicted as strange and bizarre oddities. The fact that the internees were offered generous parole and were allowed to leave the camp daily has been a particular point of wonder. However, as this chapter shows, conditions such as these were also prevalent in Switzerland, which interned far more belligerent personnel than Ireland. The de Valera government consciously modelled its internment policy on European precedents, paying particular attention to Sweden and Switzerland. At the same time, Dublin was involved in the everyday lives of prisoners of war abroad, through the sending of Red Cross parcels and personal packages to camps all over Europe.*

Keywords: employment; parcels; parole; Red Cross

Kelly, Bernard. *Military Internees, Prisoners of War and the Irish State during the Second World War.* Basingstoke: Palgrave Macmillan, 2015. DOI: 10.1057/9781137446039.0006.

DOI: 10.1057/9781137446039.0006

The 1998 film *The Brylcreem Boys*, written by Terence Ryan and starring Gabriel Byrne, is a loose depiction of life for belligerent internees within K-Lines during the Second World War. Focussing on the rivalry between a Canadian RAF pilot and an aristocratic German officer, the film is set in 1941 and contains the usual array of Irish cinematic stereotypes: bouts of fighting, soft accents, red-haired women and spontaneous displays of Irish dancing. It also neatly conveys one of the most persistent misconceptions about the belligerent internment camp at the Curragh. During an early scene, steely-eyed Captain Deegan of the Irish army arrests the main character, a Canadian pilot named Miles Keogh, and then announces solemnly that the RAF crew are in the custody of the Irish army as prisoners of war. Like the fictional Deegan, historians, journalists and other commentators consistently and erroneously have over the years compared K-Lines to prisoner of war camps and have therefore been astonished to discover the easy life of the internees in the Curragh. The aspect that attracts the most attention is parole, and the fact that belligerent internees were allowed to leave the camp on an almost daily basis is universally commented upon as being the most bizarre feature of life in the Curragh.

This consistent emphasis on K-Lines as being a cosy and comfortable place to while away the war years represents a fundamental misunderstanding of the purpose of the camp and how it should be viewed. Rather than being seen and depicted as an exceptionally liberal prisoner of war camp, it needs to be placed in its proper context alongside the belligerent internment camps run by other European neutral states, particularly Sweden and Switzerland. During the film when Keogh protests that as he has landed in a neutral country and he should not therefore be arrested, Captain Deegan snarls at him that Ireland deals with crashed fliers differently than Switzerland. The actual truth is that Switzerland was one country which assistant secretary of External Affairs Frederick Boland specifically mentioned several times as being a model upon which Dublin based its belligerent internment regime during the early phase of the war. Seen against this background, the admittedly tolerant conditions within K-Lines are not an aberration or a uniquely and typically Irish way of dealing with the situation: in fact, the camp was run along the same principles as were applied in both Sweden and Switzerland. Both countries offered extensive parole arrangements and held internees in loosely guarded confinement. Comparing K-Lines with prisoner of war camps does not offer us any useful insights, as it is not

DOI: 10.1057/9781137446039.0006

a comparison of like with like. Depending on where they were captured and who their captor was, the experiences of prisoners of war diverged wildly. Allied troops in German hands, who were by and large treated well, had a far more difficult life than the men in the Curragh, and their incarceration experiences cannot remotely be compared. The analogy becomes even more absurd when applied to Soviet prisoners in German hands, Axis prisoners held in the USSR, or Allied troops captured by the Japanese in the Far East. There is simply no way of locating belligerent internment within the 'concentration camp universe',[1] which existed in Europe during the Second World War. As Laurence Rees has observed, the variety of prisoner experience during the Second World War was unprecedented.[2] Therefore, it is only logical that internment of belligerent personnel by neutrals be removed from its current flawed context of prisoner of war incarceration.

The aim of any combatant during a war is to destroy the enemy's capacity to fight, primarily by killing, wounding or capturing members of the armed forces of its opponent. Each belligerent therefore detains as many prisoners of war as possible and guards them closely, as each prisoner taken and held represents a measurable reduction of the enemy's fighting power. The huge resources that are devoted to holding prisoners of war are justified by this fact. Niall Ferguson has suggested that warring nations make use of military prisoners in four ways: as a source of intelligence, for labour, as hostages or as an example in order to persuade other members of the enemy forces to surrender.[3] None of these categories apply to belligerent internees in Ireland or in any other neutrals during the Second World War. Although G2 questioned each airman and sailor who landed in Ireland, they were not captured for this purpose. The sole reason Dublin detained combatant personnel was to fulfil Ireland's international duty as a neutral country. Failure to intern, or displaying excessive favouritism to one over the other, would lead to questions over the validity of neutrality. This is precisely what happened from 1943 onwards when Berlin protested against the constant release of US aircrew downed in Eire. Thus, from the very beginning of the war, Dublin's motivation to detain belligerent personnel was very different from the warring powers. Although the first detainees were initially classified by the government as prisoners of war, we have already seen that this was only to allow the Irish authorities to establish a precedent for how they should be treated, and to ensure that the provisions of the Geneva Conventions could be applied to them. From October 1940

DOI: 10.1057/9781137446039.0006

onwards, once the Department of External Affairs assumed the leading role in running the camp, the internees ceased to be regarded as prisoners and were treated accordingly.

A close analysis of the conditions within K-Lines shows that restrictions were gradually eased as the Irish authorities became more and more confident in handling the internees. What is also evident is that, despite some suspicion from Irish military officers towards the belligerent personnel, the government clearly felt that there was no danger in allowing the internees to roam around the countryside and interact with Irish civilians. The parole area was steadily increased in size, which led to longer and longer hours of liberty. Visits to private houses were eventually allowed, with a few exceptions. Once the British internees departed from the Curragh in October 1943, the rules governing the remaining Germans were relaxed considerably. German personnel moved to Dublin to work in the German Legation, to attend university courses, or to find employment in the local area. None of this escaped the notice of the British government, and MI5 was kept informed about the extent of parole given to the German internees in the run-up to the invasion of Normandy.[4] The issue of paid employment became particularly important to the German internees as Germany collapsed in 1944–45, and payments for their upkeep ceased to be forwarded by Berlin.

In addition to internment camps in other neutral countries, the other most obvious parallel with K-Lines was Tintown, the internment camp which held republican detainees. Although the comparison is far from perfect, as the IRA were seen as far more dangerous and treated much more harshly by the Irish state, these internees shared the same physical space as the belligerent personnel. Both camps were located in the Curragh and were less than one mile apart. The Irish military controlled both, the O/C of the Curragh oversaw both camps and the guards rotated between the two. The relationship between the state and the IRA was one of bitter mutual hostility. During the war, five IRA members were executed by firing squad and one was hanged. Three more were allowed to die on hunger strike, while the IRA killed six members of the police during the conflict. Life in Tintown was bleak, in comparison to K-Lines. The men were kept in huts, often with 30 in each, and the lack of proper washing facilities meant that hygiene was a constant problem. Convicted IRA members were sometimes transferred to the Curragh to serve the remainder of their imprisonment, as happened with the writer Brendan Behan who arrived in September 1943 to serve out a 14-year

DOI: 10.1057/9781137446039.0006

sentence for the attempted murder of a police officer. Parole was offered to the inmates, but those who 'signed out' were ostracised and shunned by their comrades if they availed of it. The detainees themselves were split into various factions and there was continual ideological turmoil amongst the inmates. MI5 reported in May 1944 that the IRA was so riddled with splits that 'it could scarcely be described as an organisation'.[5] The tension in Tintown culminated in the shooting dead of an internee by the PAs in December 1940, following a riot and the burning of huts to protest a cut in the butter ration. There were also persistent accusations of beatings and mistreatment of internees and prisoners.[6]

When the decision was made to intern the crew of the FW-200 Condor which crashed in Kerry on 20 August 1940, no preparations had been made to receive or accommodate belligerent service personnel. However, the government could not simply release the German crew as it had been doing with the British since the start of the war; London would never agree to such a policy and therefore they had to be interned. The order to set aside K-Lines as the internment camp was not signed until 24 August,[7] four days after the Condor had crashed and then confirmed by higher authority on 28 August.[8] K-Lines consisted of a series of bungalows, which were turned over to the Germans and surrounded with barbed wire. They were quickly visited by Hempel, who provided them with board games and a radio.[9] Amongst the first internees was Oberleutnant Kurt Mollenhauer, the senior German officer, who would become a constant irritant to the camp authorities.

The lack of preparation was again highlighted once the first British pilot was detained. Flying Officer Paul Mayhew's Hurricane, having shot down a HE-111, ran out of fuel and landed in a field in Wexford on 29 September 1940. The Cabinet was notified in October 1940 that, as there was no accommodation ready for him, he was held in Ceannt barracks at the Curragh, where he was fed in the officers' mess[10] and had access to their sporting and leisure facilities. An extension to K-Lines was specially constructed for him and any future Allied internees, and he was moved to his new home on 17 October. He remained the lone Allied internee until December 1940, when five further British pilots eventually joined him. The camp now consisted of two sections, 'G' camp for the Axis and 'B' camp for the Allies,[11] which were separated by high barbed wire fences and the whole of K-Lines was further surrounded by a high fence and guard posts.

DOI: 10.1057/9781137446039.0006

In this early phase, primary responsibility for K-Lines rested with the Department of Defence and, in particular, Thomas McNally, O/C of the Curragh command. Initially both the IRA and belligerent internment camps came under the same administration, until a separate establishment was created for the belligerents only in July 1942.[12] McNally's correspondence shows that he was deeply suspicious of the belligerent internees, particularly the Germans, and he was determined not to give them any opportunity to escape. 'These prisoners' he wrote of the Luftwaffe crew on 12 September 1940,

> are the type who consider it a duty to escape at the first available opportunity. As a race they are very thorough and methodical and I feel they will avail themselves of any laxity in the regulations which govern their internment. (Irish Military Archives, S/231, McNally to O'hAodh, 12 September 1940)

As a precaution, he had men stationed in the internees living quarters in order to prevent any tunnelling.[13] He ordered that the gardening tools, which were given to the German internees as recreation, be collected from them every night. Because of the fear of escape, they were not allowed to travel to Dublin to visit their Legation, but consular visits were to be unsupervised.[14] He further refused to let them have alcohol.

Following complaints from the German minister, Boland wrote to Liam Archer of G2, urging a reduction in the security surrounding K-Lines and suggesting that, rather than a strict list of rules being drawn up, that internee issues be tackled as they arose.[15] In his reply, Archer admitted that McNally had been over zealous in guarding the internees and that the military had inadvertently been applying the same security to the belligerent internees as to the IRA detainees:

> I personally thought that our difficulty in handling these internees was due to the fact that we had hitherto been compelled to exercise a somewhat rigid control on the freedom of the internees we had hitherto been responsible for. We had, furthermore, no previous experience of handling internees of the belligerent class and accordingly it was conceivable we might unconsciously be applying to these German internees our regulations regarding internees of Irish nationality. (Irish Military Archives, S/231, Archer to O'hAodh, 6 September, 1940)

The solution, Archer continued, was to ease off the restrictions and to allow the belligerent internees as much freedom as was possible, without allowing them to escape. In his opinion, keeping them 'as contented with their lot here as possible' would 'minimise their anxiety and quite natural desire to escape from our custody'. The best way to do this was by

DOI: 10.1057/9781137446039.0006

'keeping their minds occupied and in keeping their bodies healthy and thereby reduce the monotony of their confinement.'[16]

Despite resistance from McNally, who appears to have taken this decision as a personal rebuke, from this point on there was a gradual loosening of restrictions in K-Lines. In a letter to O'hAodh in January 1941, McNally protested that he was under 'adverse criticism' from External Affairs, but that he understood that belligerent internees were to be treated differently and much more leniently than the IRA. 'It was explained at great length' he complained,

> that these men were not to be considered Internees in the sense that we look upon Internees in No.1 camp. Analogous conditions in Switzerland were also explained in detail with a view to showing that there was not the necessity for a great deal of rigour, and in fact the maximum concessions should be made consistent with precautions against their attempting to escape.[17]

The most important of these concessions was parole. This was left at McNally's discretion, but it was clear that the authorities were eager to grant it. McNally was told by de Valera himself in June 1941 that the internees were 'to be treated with the utmost friendliness and to be permitted the greatest liberty in the matter of parole.'[18] In November 1941 it was again stressed that 'the internees should be facilitated to the utmost in the granting of parole.'[19] At a conference in November 1940, it was agreed that the German internees would be allowed to exercise outside their compound and to visit the cinema, upon applying for parole in writing.[20] Under instructions issued by the Air Ministry in February 1940, Mayhew was not allowed to accept any form of parole unless he was specifically ordered otherwise.[21] However, McNally suggested that he could still leave the camp if he gave his 'personal word of honour' not to escape, as he was basically living in B camp by himself. Even if Mayhew was not prepared to do this, McNally was willing to allow him to leave the camp under armed escort. It was further noted that Mayhew's father, who had travelled to Ireland, should be allowed to visit.[22]

Eventually, after trial and error, three types of parole were formalised and offered to the internees. Camp parole allowed them to leave their compound and remain within the Curragh complex, for the purposes of exercise, 'collective recreating, bathing, route marches' and related activities. This was offered between the hours of nine in the morning to five in the evening and an undertaking had to be signed by the senior internee. Local parole gave internees the opportunity to explore the countryside surrounding the camp, up to a maximum of a ten-mile radius, although this was adjusted as the war went on to take in more villages and towns. Men on local parole had to be in possession of a pass and sign out at the guard hut at the entrance to K-Lines. The final type was special parole, which was granted to internees who wished to travel to Dublin. Before leaving the camp, internees had to sign their parole form, which stated that while they were outside the wire, they would not

> make or endeavour to make any arrangements whatever to seek or accept any assistance whatever with a view to the escape of myself or my fellow internees, that I will not engage in any military activity or activities contrary to the interests of Éire, and that I will not go outside the permitted area.[23]

This formula was based on the Swedish model and drafted by External Affairs after Boland had studied the parole forms offered by the Swedish military to their belligerent internees.[24]

It is uncertain when the British government reversed its policy on parole, but reports from McNally show Mayhew asking to be allowed to visit Dublin to go shopping in November 1940[25] and by the end of January 1941, new parole conditions were put in place for both sets of internees. By now the camp was filling up rapidly and by the end of March 1941, there were sixteen British and fifteen Germans.[26] Each group were allowed out to play golf, to swim or to attend religious services. They were also permitted to attend the cinema in the village of Newbridge, or to go shopping in the local area, but remained at all times under escort.[27] Germans and British were paroled at separate times: Germans were allowed to visit the cinema in Newbridge on Wednesday and Sunday, the Allied internees on Tuesday and Saturday.[28] When leaving the camp, internees undertook by to return by a certain time and dress in civilian attire when signing their parole form. The German Legation paid for clothes for its internees, while the British personnel bought their own clothing, and also wore some that were donated by the British Legion.[29] McNally insisted that, while outside the camp, internees were not to visit private houses or pubs, and would be under escort the entire time. This irritated both sets of internees, who felt that since they had signed their parole forms and pledged not to escape while outside, they did not need to be watched. However, McNally pointed out that the escorts were not there to spy on the internees, but instead to 'ensure that no subversive elements will interfere with them'.[30]

DOI: 10.1057/9781137446039.0006

In May 1941, after a further influx of internees, the Provost Marshal reviewed the situation in K-Lines. B camp now consisted of one bunga-low and one hut, each containing bedrooms, separate sitting rooms for officers and NCOs, a recreational room, bathrooms and shower rooms. G camp was made up of five bungalows with a total capacity of 32, but both camps were ready for expansion. Parole and other recreation had also settled into a pattern:

> Internees are granted parole for exercise purposes each day from 14.00 to 17.00 hours. They have permission during these periods to play golf at the Curragh Golf Links and tennis at the Command Tennis club. Parole is granted 3 mornings weekly for the purpose of swimming in the Camp Swimming Baths and also on four evenings weekly to facilitate the internees visiting the Picture Houses at Newbridge and the Curragh Camp. Table Tennis equip-ment is available and Wireless sets are installed in both Camps.[31]

It was around this time that local people began to offer the use of horses to the internees,[32] and in June 1941 McNally agreed to this, with the proviso that they were not allowed to go hunting. Parole conditions were further eased at this meeting; the area was now extended to include the town of Naas, internees could attend local dances and visits to local houses were now permitted, as long as there were no 'demonstrations by local residents of sympathy with any particular side'. Emphasising the ever-present diplomatic aspects of the camp, all these concessions were subject to confirmation by de Valera himself. McNally, however, felt that the new conditions would present no difficulties, given that the internees had been 'accepted by the local inhabitants'.[33]

It is concessions such as these which have caused past writers to comment on the strange nature of the camp. However, the liberties that the men in K-Lines enjoyed were replicated in belligerent intern-ment camps in Switzerland. Here interned US airmen were kept in small isolated Alpine villages such as Adelboden, Neuchatel, Wengen and Davos, where they were accommodated in hotels and were able to supplement the Swiss army rations they received by purchasing food in local restaurants.[34] Like those held in Ireland, Allied internees passed the time by playing board games, visiting the cinema, sport, photography and mingling with the locals. Internees in Switzerland also spent a good deal of time learning to ski.[35] By a strange quirk of fate, the internee hotel in Davos was located directly across the street from the German Legation.[36] One American internee recalled that he was permitted to

DOI: 10.1057/9781137446039.0006

travel to Zurich on a day pass and, in his opinion, if more travel had been allowed, there would have been considerably less trouble in the camps.[37]

At the same time, although the Irish government had no control or influence over how Irish prisoners of war were treated in Axis camps, Dublin still inadvertently became involved in their daily lives. One of the lifelines that prisoners of war clung to were Red Cross parcels and packages from home. Once Germany began to collapse in 1945 and prisoners of war were sent on long, meandering marches to avoid being liberated, Red Cross parcels could quite literally be life saving,[38] and authors have depicted desperate and hungry prisoners fighting over them in the last months of the war.[39] Although they had not given it any thought prior to the outbreak of war, despite the large number of Irish in the British forces, the de Valera government was forced to establish a policy on the sending of parcels and correspondence to prisoners of war abroad, as it soon became clear that many Irish families had a member in Axis captivity, or wanted to send parcels to prisoners of other nationalities held abroad. Due to the lack of any forward thinking, it took until 1943 for a package sending scheme to be established, and then only after much discussion, and disagreement. In addition, the Department of External Affairs was soon fielding many queries from Irish citizens, anxious for any information about their loved ones. The response to both of these issues was largely improvised and, although some patterns can be identified, the government generally reacted to situation as they arose. Their advice to families of prisoners of war was often erratic and contradictory.

The life of the men in K-Lines became intertwined with Dublin's lack of policy on correspondence and parcels for prisoners of war held abroad in 1943. There were two types of parcels sent to prisoners during the Second World War: official Red Cross packages and 'next-of-kin' parcels, which were sent by the families but vetted and repackaged by the Red Cross. As the Irish Red Cross did not independently send parcels to Irish prisoners abroad, the 'next-of-kin' package was the one most often sent from Ireland. The Society did, however, send packages to prisoners of other nationalities and to the internees in the Curragh. In December 1939 the Irish Red Cross contacted External Affairs requesting information on how to send parcels to German prisoners in British hands; de Valera neatly sidestepped this issue by suggesting that they forward the query to the International Red Cross in Switzerland.[40] In January 1940, the Department of Posts and Telegraphs circulated instructions to

DOI: 10.1057/9781137446039.0006

all post offices on how to handle correspondence for prisoners of war, based on information sent to Dublin by the Dominions Office.

Following this, Posts and Telegraphs asked External Affairs if it was feasible to follow the British example and establish a free parcel-sending process in Eire, with the assistance of the Irish Red Cross, but this was vetoed by Michael Rynne in August 1941. He suggested that the government becoming directly involved in the sending of prisoner parcels was 'undesirable from the political point of view', and he felt that the present system of referring all queries to the British Red Cross as the best available option.[41] Rynne's allusion to the 'political point of view' undoubtedly referred to neutrality and the publicity that might attach to the sending of parcels to Irish members of the British forces. The same caution was evident when the Irish Red Cross suggested cooperating with the Yugoslav government in exile to send food packages, purchased in Ireland, to Yugoslav prisoners in German custody; Boland replied that while the de Valera had no objection to the plan, other government departments needed to be consulted and 'matters of this kind are more appropriately dealt with between the National Red Cross Societies themselves', rather than the government.[42] In July 1943, the Irish Red Cross agreed to send food packages to Polish prisoners of war in Germany; one of the oddest aspects of this scheme was that while Ireland provided the food, the government had to obtain the sanction of the British Ministry of Food to secure cans to send it in. Empty food tins were supplied by London on the understanding that they would be used to send food to the UK only, which emphasised both the food situation in Britain and the lack of manufacturing in Ireland.[43] The parcels, packed with butter, milk, stewed steak and corned beef, eventually reached the International Red Cross in February 1944.[44]

Their willingness to assist prisoners of war in Europe notwithstanding, one matter which the de Valera government showed a marked reluctance to become involved in was sending packages to Irish prisoners of war directly. As already noted, Dublin had no legal standing to intervene on behalf of Irish members of the Allied forces, regardless of how they were treated in Axis captivity. When approached by relatives, External Affairs invariably recommended that they direct their concerns to the Irish Red Cross. When the Irish Legation in Berlin was asked in late 1944 if the Irish Red Cross was interested in sending food parcels directly to Irish prisoners in Germany, in addition to any they might receive from other sources, the Irish Chargé d'Affaires in Berlin, Con Cremin, explained

DOI: 10.1057/9781137446039.0006

that they were cared for by the British Red Cross and Nicholas Nolan at External Affairs confirmed that Dublin was not going to take the matter further.[45] Presumably this was to avoid allegations of unneutral behaviour, but it might also attract unwelcome attention to the number of Irish in the British forces. However, External Affairs sanctioned the sending of parcels through the Irish Red Cross to individual prisoners of various other nationalities, and in August 1943 Walshe confirmed that this included Axis prisoners held in the UK. Some had already been sent 'without any difficulty or question of principle arising'.[46] Although it may sound harsh, this was undoubtedly the correct attitude for a neutral to adopt, as Dublin could not claim to be outside the conflict but also directly favouring Irish prisoners of war. The memoirs of Jack Harte, a Dubliner who was captured while serving in the British forces in the Mediterranean, make clear that he and his British comrades received Red Cross parcels, although the frequency of their arrival was irregular. In Jack's case, he recalled that they came from the Canadian Red Cross.[47]

One of the major problems faced by relatives of Irish prisoners of war was that, as Dublin had signed but never actually ratified the 1929 Geneva Convention, Irish civilians had to pay the cost of sending correspondence to camps, while inhabitants of those countries which had adopted the Convention could send them free of charge. As Irish parcels were generally routed through Britain, this meant that the majority of senders had only to pay postage from Ireland to the UK but, as the Irish Red Cross Society pointed out in September 1942, in some cases even this relatively small cost was hard to bear for some families, particularly if parcels were sent regularly or in multiples. In some cases, Irish prisoners of war were in desperate need. In early 1941, the Irish Red Cross received letters from Irish prisoners in Germany, stating that their British comrades had received parcels, but that Irish prisoners did not. In reply, the Red Cross informed the unfortunate men that personal parcels had to be routed through the British Red Cross, which had responsibility for all members of the British forces.[48]

Parcels to other Irish abroad – civilians interned in Germany, for example – had to be sent directly to the Red Cross in Geneva, which resulted in significant financial outlay on even a small bundle.[49] There were around 150 Irish citizens in Europe who had been released from internment and who were being supported by Eire diplomatic representatives. In the case of a Waterford man who had been interned in Germany as a member of the British merchant navy, but subsequently

DOI: 10.1057/9781137446039.0006

released, neither the government nor his family were able even to send him a package of new clothing. The Red Cross could not assist him as he was no longer classified as a prisoner of war, and the British government refused to allow the shipment of parcels to non-internees, as 'there can be no guarantee that clothing will not be diverted by the enemy to other purposes'.[50] The Irish Red Cross urged the government to ratify the postal sections of the 1929 Convention, in order to assist Irish civilians, internees and prisoners of war.

The other major obstacle facing those who wished to send packages abroad was the wartime censorship of correspondence. Staff in Posts and Telegraphs did not examine packages which were forwarded by Irish civilians to the British or International Red Cross, as they knew the parcels would be opened and repacked, and any prohibited items removed by the charitable societies abroad. The list of banned objects was formidable. Articles that would be useful in escapes, such as binoculars or compasses were obvious, but also forbidden were complete suits, mirrors, candles, books, cigarettes and certain types of food.[51] There were consistent complaints from the postal authorities in the UK that parcels from Ireland were either incorrectly packed or were full of banned items, a situation which would have been avoided if the government had addressed the issue and sent clear guidelines to the public sooner. Michael Rynne at External Affairs suggested that the Irish Red Cross collect items for prisoners and despatch parcels independently of Britain, but ran into resistance from both Post and Telegraphs and the Red Cross itself, both of whom objected that they did not have the staff to open and examine each individual package. As Rynne noted, the issue 'bristles with minor difficulties'.[52]

Assistant secretary of External Affairs Frederick Boland had a much more straightforward view of the problem. Writing to Rynne on 14 January 1941, he dismissed the Irish Red Cross objections entirely:

> If the Irish Red Cross is going to be a proper national Society and not a mere sub-agency of the British Society, it must accustom itself to undertaking this sort of work. I cannot understand why there should be any difficulty about getting volunteers to examine and repack these parcels. If there are people in this country, as we know there are, willing to make up the parcels, attend knitting classes to make comforts for the troops, etc., why should it be impossible to recruit a voluntary staff which, working under the supervision of an officer from the Censor's office, would undertake the necessary examination and repacking work... They should be told that this is the kind of work that

DOI: 10.1057/9781137446039.0006

they were set up to do and that, if they drop into the habit of constantly looking to the British Society and conducting their international contacts through
them, they might as well not be here at all. (National Archives of Ireland,
DFA 241/126. Boland to Rynne, 14 January 1941)

Furthermore, the clearly irritated Boland contended that although Ireland
had not ratified the 1929 Convention, it had still signed it and was therefore
morally, if not strictly legally, bound to abide by its provisions. Therefore
Dublin should allow the families of prisoners to send parcels free of
charge, with the cost being borne by the Irish State.[53] At the root of his
annoyance was the fact that he hated 'the idea of referring our own citizens
to the British Red Cross Society when we have a Red Cross Society of our
own'.[54] Rynne agreed with these sentiments: writing to R.J. Cremins, the
assistant secretary at the Department of Posts and Telegraphs, he lamented
the fact that the government had to become involved at all, but the hoped-
for assistance from the Irish Red Cross 'did not materialise and does not
seem likely to materialise within any appreciable time'.[55] In one celebrated
example, local people in Kerry took matters into their own hands. In
July 1943, a British flying boat carrying letters from British prisoners in
Japanese captivity crashed into Mount Brandon, scattering thousands of
letters across the mountainside. Locals who came upon the scene helped
the survivors and also pieced together many of the letters before posting
them through ordinary mail to the intended recipients in Britain.[56]

Because of the lack of any preparation for the matter, it was not until
February 1943 that the Department of Finance sanctioned the creation
of a free-parcel scheme,[57] which came about after long and complex
negotiations between the government departments. The Department
of Supplies, headed by Sean Lemass, agreed to issue an extra 75 clothing coupons, as well as extra soap, for next-of-kin to send to prisoners
of war 'on the condition that both the next-of-kin and the prisoner of
war were Irish nationals'.[58] Tragically, many parcels sent to prisoners in
Japanese custody were never delivered to the camps, or arrived years
after dispatch, or were plundered by the camp guards.[59]

One of the reasons why the negotiations between the departments
took so long was that the issue of correspondence for prisoners of war
abroad became entangled with the matter of sending parcels to the
belligerent internees in the Curragh. The draft instructions issued by
the Department of Posts and Telegraphs included instructions on sending personal packages to 'prisoners interned in Eire or in the United
Kingdom' through the Irish Red Cross, and detailed a long list of items

that were prohibited.[60] Secretary of the Department of Defence, Peadar MacMahon, objected to this, pointing out that the internees in K-Lines were held under Emergency Powers Order no. 170 and 'the description "prisoners of war" is not properly applicable to them'. He also noted that, unlike prisoners of war, no restrictions were placed on items posted to the belligerent internees, that the camp authorities would examine all packages received and therefore there was no need to send correspondence via the Irish Red Cross. He finally suggested that a new section be inserted to the Posts and Telegraphs pamphlet dealing specifically with post to K-Lines.[61] An External Affairs note in February 1943 agreed with the point that internees were in a special category and 'not (strictly speaking) prisoners of war at all'.[62] Boland concurred, confirming that 'internees in neutral countries are not prisoners of war and it is wrong to refer to them as such'.[63] Rynne suggested omitting the belligerent internees entirely from any postal arrangement,[64] and the Bureau of Information let it be known that they did not want the public to know they could send any items they wished to the men in the Curragh. 'Scarcely any citizens are piling gifts on the internees at the moment' wrote Rynne, 'and it is not desired to start any such ramp.'[65] G2 further reinforced this attitude and, as Rynne noted, military intelligence certainly did not

> welcome the prospect of dealing with a "fan mail" from the "Friends of Germany" and their British counterparts. The present censorship staff could scarcely cope with the extra work, apart from the political aspects of the thing which the Department of Defence feel are objectionable.[66]

The leaflet eventually issued to the public made no mention of post to the internment camps in the Curragh. Rynne felt that the instructions were unbalanced as they referred to people 'in the custody of the Tripartite Powers' only, but hoped that this and 'Other unavoidable anomalies arising out of the one-sided nature of the present arrangements have been concealed as well as possible in the final draft'.[67] This was unavoidable as the majority of prisoner correspondence leaving Ireland was for Irish members of the British forces in Axis captivity.

Despite the official reluctance, the belligerent internees in K-Lines did not have any issues with receiving parcels and a steady stream of gifts and letters flowed into their camp, most of them consisting of clothing, food and alcohol. G2 was well aware that German internees were evading the regulations by posting letters while out on parole,[68] but External Affairs pointed out that censorship in K-Lines was based on the model Sweden

DOI: 10.1057/9781137446039.0006

imposed on its belligerent internees.[69] In addition, the Irish Society of Friends requested and received permission to send sports equipment to the German internees, although Peadar MacMahon cautioned the donors that items would be distributed to all the internees as equally as possible:[70] some may have been given to the Allied internees. Lists of donations from the German Legation in November 1940 contain portraits of Hitler and Göring, books, wine, chocolate, cigarettes, sausages, fruit, brandy, champagne and whiskey,[71] all of which was carefully recorded by G2.[72] The Allied internees received their own fair share of gifts, including a piano from the Cementation Company in county Kildare.[73]

Various Red Cross societies also forwarded care packages to the military internees during the conflict. The German Red Cross sent parcels of vitamins,[74] while the Irish society sent annual food hampers at Christmastime. For example, in December 1942, both B and G camps received 12 bottles of whiskey, three turkeys and two hams.[75] The British Red Cross regularly sent clothing to the Allied internees, but the most frequent and most welcome deliveries were of cigarettes. Records in the Irish Military Archives show a constant flow of cigarettes being delivered by the British and German societies. After the British internees were released and the German Legation fell into financial difficulty, the Irish Red Cross sent supplies of tobacco to the Germans; for example in December 1944 the senior internee officer acknowledged receipt of 2,000 cigarettes at camp no. 1B.[76]

However, there were many complaints from the internees regarding the conditions in K-Lines. In January 1941, the Allied internees submitted a long list of grievances, including the standard of hygiene in their kitchen, the lack of variety in the diet, the shortage of bathing facilities and a desire for more furniture.[77] In February 1942, they protested against a lack of fuel for their rooms and washing facilities[78] and in 1943 they suspected that fleas had infested the huts, which was investigated and rejected by the army medical service.[79] The indefatigable Mollenhauer, on the other hand, wrote to the army authorities so often criticising G camp that McNally described him as a 'somewhat neurotic' person who made 'interminable complaints about the conditions of internment.'[80] Like the Allied internees, he too complained about the lack of fuel in October 1941, whereupon he was informed that his men had received twice the amount allowed to Irish army officers.[81] He would later object to articles in the Irish Defence Forces journal, *An Cosantóir*, delays in posting internee letters, the showing of British war films in the Curragh

DOI: 10.1057/9781137446039.0006

cinema, the lack of proper cleaning brushes and cloths in the German huts and the scarcity of furniture in their rooms. On this last point, Boland noted that the International Red Cross had set a standard level for officers furnishings in prisoner of war camps, and he felt that Dublin 'would be wise not to give either set of belligerents any ground for valid complaint on this score'.[82]

Because the Curragh was a long-established military town, many retired soldiers and officers had settled in the area surrounding the camp and once the internees had received permission to visit local houses, they were soon in demand for social events. Initially, they had to request special parole for this, and this was usually granted provided that the men agreed to return to the camp by 8 AM. From that point on, Allied internees simply applied for the 8 AM deadline every time they signed out, without needing to have a specified event to attend.[83] The first overnight parole, meaning that he did not have to return to sign back in, was granted in April 1942 to a British internee whose wife had come to Ireland to visit, and this was soon extended to all internees whose wives were in the parole area.[84]

Boland's aim in allowing as much leniency as possible to the internees was to avoid any incidents at the camp. Given that the opposing internees lived in such close proximity to each other, there was always the potential for trouble. However, Boland's policy proved to be the correct one because there were very few incidents between both sets of internees. In December 1942, the Germans sent the Allies a Christmas gift of wine and a cake, but it took the personal intervention of an Irish officer to persuade the men in B camp to accept it and reciprocate, sending several bottles of brandy.[85] The most serious occurrence was a brief fight between two Germans and a Polish RAF pilot named Jan Zimek after a dance in May 1943, in which Zimek was injured when punched off his bicycle by one of the Germans. Despite one author dramatically and completely erroneously claiming that Zimek was almost killed by the Germans,[86] the official report stated that while he may have had a fracture, he was not 'in any immediate danger of death'.[87] He was shortly thereafter transferred to Northern Ireland on compassionate grounds, although the real reason was that Boland feared Zimek would cause trouble if he were to return to K-Lines.[88] Following this, both sets of internees were allowed out on parole until three o' clock daily, but after 3 PM parole was curtailed and each were permitted to leave only on alternate days.[89] Both the Allied and German minister agreed to this, and the Allied internees accepted the decision 'philosophically', but Mollenhauer was 'troublesome' when informed. Maffey and Hempel took the opportunity to press de Valera to establish separate camps.[90]

De Valera's decision to release 20 of the Allied internees in October 1943, with the remaining eleven also being set free in June 1944, largely removed the diplomatic aspect of internment and meant that the problems that remained were relatively routine. Even when issues did arise, as with the internment of the German sailors in January 1944, Hempel was unable to influence government policy and, with the war clearly going against them, Germany had little or no ability to pressurise Dublin. Once the decision to release the Allies was confirmed, a new camp was constructed at Gormanstown, named No.4 internment camp, which was opened towards the end of October 1943. The 11 men who were housed there had parole every day until 8 AM, whereupon they generally returned to sign in before leaving the camp again. Several of them joined local sports clubs and played football with the Irish army.[91]

Around the same time, a total of 18 German internees were eventually granted permission to live in Dublin, where they began courses in University College Dublin and the College of Technology. They were given strict instructions to live in groups, be indoors by midnight, avoid all transport hubs and military barracks. They were also to keep away from places such as the Gresham Hotel, the Dolphin Hotel and the Hibernian Buttery, in order to avoid 'disputes or troublesome incidents;' although it was not stated in the documents, this was undoubtedly to avoid Allied troops, as all three establishments were popular with service personnel on leave in the capital. Most importantly of all, they were not to make contact with any political groups or associations.[92] This also applied to the internees still in the camp. There appears to have been no interaction between the German internees and the pro-Axis scene in Ireland during the war. The only recorded incident was when one of the naval internees was invited to lunch by Dan Breen, a veteran of the 1919–21 revolution against British rule and Fianna Fáil TD for Tipperary. Permission for the visit was swiftly denied. Although the stated reason was that the internee was neither an officer nor an NCO, and therefore not allowed parole in Dublin,[93] the real motive was probably to avoid the embarrassment of having a German serviceman taken to lunch by a member of de Valera's own parliamentary party. Always an opinionated and tactless individual, Breen made no secret of his anti-British views, and was known to be pro-Axis during the war.[94] Breen was also observed

DOI: 10.1057/9781137446039.0006

by the Gardaí making frequent visits to German officials in Dublin during the war,[95] so it is little wonder that the authorities found a reason to stop German internees visiting him. In a famous example of how much liberty the internees actually had, in 1945 two sailors apologised for breaking parole as they had been sailing in Dublin bay;[96] on 2 January the senior internee himself had to write a contrite note of apology as he had slept in 'after a very hard celebration' and missed the bus back to the Curragh.[97]

For the Germans remaining in K-Lines, life became far more complicated by the arrival of the 164 German sailors rescued in January 1944. As there was not enough room at K-Lines to accommodate the new internees, the decision was made to open a new camp adjacent to the IRA compound at the Curragh, which was designated internment camp No. 1B[98] but is also sometimes called No.2A.[99] (Other letters simply refer to it as camp No.1). This opened on 25 January 1944, first for the sailors only, before the Luftwaffe internees were transferred from K-Lines in March. A combination of the cramped conditions, a precarious supply situation and Germany's increasingly hopeless position meant that morale in the new camp slumped badly. Instead of bungalows, as in K-Lines, the new camp contained eight huts that were divided into cubicles for the men as well as recreation spaces, an office and washrooms. McNally acknowledged that space was at a premium and warned shortly after the men were moved that there was only space for four more internees.[100] To both McNally's and Boland's great relief, Mollenhauer had to relinquish the role of senior internee to Kaptaenleutnant Joachim Quedenfeld, the highest-ranking naval internee. However, he was less than impressed when he inspected the new camp and he complained in February 1944 that it was too damp and too many men were held there, even before the arrival of the Luftwaffe personnel. McNally attributed his attitude to the negative influence of both Hempel and Mollenhauer.[101]

Fuel shortages in Ireland further added to the problems in the camp. At a conference in January 1944, it was decided that no more coal could be provided to the internees and instead only wood or turf would be supplied.[102] By 1944 the shortage of coal in Ireland was acute, partly due to restricted supply from the Allied countries. The Defence Forces, who had been supplying the internees with fuel, had seen its coal reserve cut in half to a mere 6748 tons, all of which was distributed to the various commands by March 1944.[103] In September 1944 the camp was provided with a ration of timber when none was available for the Defence Forces to use.[104] Parole

DOI: 10.1057/9781137446039.0006

was a further concern. Now that the number of Germans had risen so sharply, Boland was unsure whether the same parole conditions could be offered to the naval internees as enjoyed by the pilots. Luftwaffe officers could remain outside the camp until 8 AM, and NCOs had to return by 5 PM.[105] Of particular concern to the government was the grant of parole to the sailors to visit Dublin. The British government was hardly likely to approve of such large groups of German officers and NCOs roaming around Dublin freely. There was also the issue of the Luftwaffe men who had been granted permission to live in Dublin to study at UCD, and Boland suggested that de Valera be consulted before the same privilege was extended to the sailors. News of German defeats, as well as the attempt on Hitler's life on 20 July 1944, depressed the mood in the camp further and the absence of the Allied internees was a constant reminder that the war was going badly for Germany. The list of incidents began to grow: several of the internees appeared in the District Court charged with stealing timber and a local woman alleged that an internee had attempted to enter her house late at night.[106] On New Year's Day 1945 some internees threw stones and broke windows in the camp after listening to an address by Hitler.[107] Hitler's speech had urged his followers to resist until the bitter end, before blaming his European allies, amongst other groups, for Germany's precarious military position.[108] There was, as Ian Kershaw has pointed out, nothing new in this sort of rhetoric, but it was enough, when combined with the frustrations of being interned, to spark a reaction from the sailors. In May 1945, following the German surrender, the PAs had to intervene to prevent the internees from attacking one of their own men.[109] At the same time, the German officers requested that they be transferred away from the camp, as they felt a 'Communist element' had taken over and they feared for their own safety and as a result, PAs were deployed to patrol within the camp itself.[110] This trouble died away within a few days following a threat by the camp commandant that all parole would be cancelled, but it was symptomatic of the ugly mood within the internment camp as the war drew to an end. The naval ratings were not the last Germans to arrive. In March 1945, the 48-strong crew of U-260 landed in Cork after their submarine struck a mine off the Fastnet Rock and were interned, adding to the crowded atmosphere. G2 recovered a large cache of documents and Enigma codebooks, which were shared with MI5.[111] On 5 May, the last German aircrew of the war landed in Ireland when a JU-88 alighted at Gormanstown aerodrome and the crew of five surrendered to the Irish authorities.[112]

DOI: 10.1057/9781137446039.0006

Germany's slow collapse had a direct financial impact on the lives of the men still interned. Already in 1941, Berlin suggested that the internees wear their uniforms while on local parole, in order to cut down on clothing costs. Boland noted that neither the men themselves nor Hempel seemed particularly keen on this idea.[113] In April 1943, the Department of Defence noted that the internees were struggling financially and were attempting to make toys to sell to the locals.[114] The German Legation in Dublin began to run out of funds in January 1944, meaning that it had difficulty in providing funding for the internees and Dublin had to step into the gap. Hempel asked External Affairs to provide the men with some money, and Boland reported that they had been given sums ranging from £2 for officers to 15 shillings for NCOs and men. In return, Boland suggested that Berlin forward credits in Swiss francs through Geneva. External Affairs also undertook to provide them with civilian clothes, although there was some consternation when McNally reported that the Luftwaffe internees had close to £1100 spare cash from selling handmade toys at Christmas and a refund from the Revenue Commissioners.[115] Furthermore, it was later discovered that the internees were selling their clothes to locals,[116] as well as selling alcohol, which they could purchase duty-free.[117] Berlin issued the internees with a final lump sum of two months pay in March 1945 and, although External Affairs knew that there would be no more forthcoming from Germany, Dublin refused to assume responsibility for the men's wages.[118] The government did undertake to pay for English classes for the internees, as Boland had discovered that other neutral countries had subsidised the education of their military internees, and he also suggested allowing up to £20 for stationary. The Irish Red Cross was asked to provide beer and cigarettes to the men,[119] and the Irish army had previously donated toiletries and collected small sums of money for the sailors.[120]

The lack of any income meant that many German internees began to look for employment outside the camp. The use of prisoners of war for labour was widespread during the First World War, due to the conscription of workers[121] and whereas the belligerent countries actively sought to utilise prisoner of war labour to plug manpower gaps, German internees seeking work in Ireland during the Second World War raised some thorny issues for the government. Britain became heavily dependant on prisoner labour, with 350,000 German prisoners working in the UK economy in 1946.[122] That same appetite for workers drew in many jobless Irish and, although Eire suffered from high unemployment during the

DOI: 10.1057/9781137446039.0006

war, it would undoubtedly have been much higher had emigration to the UK been blocked: between 1941 and 1945, 172,574 travel permits to the UK were issued by External Affairs, and the government took steps to ensure that it was only the unemployed who left.[123] However, the de Valera government had no desire to use the belligerent internees for labour and there were misgivings about allowing the internees, many of whom were skilled workers, to find jobs while many thousands of Irish citizens remained unemployed and tens of thousands were emigrating annually. There was also resistance in the locality towards the men working. In 1943, Hempel agreed that if internees found jobs through local labour exchanges, they first had to provide a certificate confirming that no Irish person was available for the job.[124] The Gardaí reported during April 1943 that the employment of internees was causing dissatisfaction amongst the 'local labour organisations' and advised that internees not be permitted to work outside camp.[125] In January 1944 the Chief of Staff of the Defence Forces opposed the idea of internees working for the Army because of the 'possibility of undesirable contacts being created'[126] and in the summer of 1944, the Department of Industry and Commerce refused to allow the internees take part in a job scheme to help with the harvest,[127] although it was satisfied to allow the internees to work in other employments in the locality.[128]

One of the more complex problems posed by the fact that the Germans wanted to work was the interpretation of the 1929 Convention on Prisoners of War. In this, the detaining power was responsible for the working conditions of prisoners, even if they worked outside the camp, but External Affairs was wary of intervening with private employers who hired German personnel. At the same time, Rynne deduced that the Convention prevented Dublin from simply ignoring its responsibility for the men once they walked out the camp gate. The only alternative, in his view, was to make a separate arrangement with Berlin regarding the internees.[129] As with other issues regarding the belligerent personnel, Dublin attempted to keep track of the policies of other neutrals. External Affairs preserved an article from the *Daily Telegraph* in March 1944 regarding the employment of British personnel in Switzerland. The article reported that the Swiss government had attempted to provide work for those who wanted it, while still giving priority to Swiss labour, which was precisely the same as the Irish approach.[130] Likewise, the Swedish regulations on internee employment were consulted. Sweden allowed internees to work outside of camp, but the authorities reserved

DOI: 10.1057/9781137446039.0006

the right to charge the internee for food, accommodation and tools if necessary.[131]

The abrupt halt in their wages forced many of the internees to seek employment independently. Reporting on the matter in April 1945 Sean Collins-Powell, who had replaced McNally, wrote that

> Since the stoppage of pay there is a general desire for work. As far as can be ascertained, however, the big majority are not desirous of manual work and prefer to participate in Handicrafts. On this point I wish to refer to the efforts made to obtain employment in various part of the COUNTRY. Another investigation revealed that some of the Internees were already engaged in casual or semi-permanent employment within the parole area. The full details of this are difficult to ascertain because neither the employer nor employee are willing to give information. (Irish Military Archives, CP 1737, Collins-Powell to Provost Marshall, 24 April 1945)

Collins-Powell preferred to keep the internees working as a group, as he felt they would be too difficult to track and control if they were to source employment individually.[132] Hempel, on the other hand, counselled against this, warning that there may be friction over the division of any profits if they were forced to work together.[133] G2, which kept a close watch on the men themselves and those they corresponded with,[134] suspected that the internees were using parole to work casually in the area, which camp regulations forbade them to do without prior permission from the camp commandant. After an investigation, it was found that 52 internees were working within the local parole area.[135] Collins-Powell recommended against allowing the Germans to find employment in case of 'repercussions from local labour'.[136] His caution was stemmed from an incident in July 1944; local workers in Kileenthomas threatened to go on strike if the Turf Development Board did not discontinue the employment of German internees in the bog. Given the crippling shortage of fuel in the country, the managers felt they had no option but to send the Germans back to the camp to avoid a work stoppage.[137] The issue became particularly acute in May 1945 after the surrender of Germany. There was no longer a German government to look after the internees and the Legation in Dublin was closed down. De Valera was 'anxious that those of the internees who are in a position to work should be allowed to do so', given that there was no other source of income available to them. Writing to the Department of Industry and Commerce in May 1945, Boland pointed out that some of the Germans were highly skilled naval mechanics who should be able to

DOI: 10.1057/9781137446039.0006

find some employment.[138] Eventually, the majority of the internees found employment in some capacity, either working within the camp, hired by private individuals around the Curragh, cutting turf or creating items such as toys and Christmas cards.

Conclusion

Because K-Lines has consistently been misidentified as a prisoner of war camp, its liberal environment has always been portrayed as a strange and bizarre phenomenon. It is true that the military internees enjoyed a relatively comfortable incarceration, with the bulk of their time spent outside the wire, but that was also true of internees in other European neutrals, particularly Switzerland. No meaningful comparison can be drawn with prisoner of war camps, as the two institutions were completely different from each other, with different rules and different motivations for holding those detained in them. Quite apart from that, the Irish government had solid, practical reasons for offering belligerent internees such liberal conditions, and absence of any serious incidents between the men demonstrates that it was the correct path to follow.

Firstly, it was in the interests of the Irish military guarding the camp and the Irish government to keep the internees happy, healthy and occupied. Morale was a constant concern for the officers in charge of the camp and they strove to keep the atmosphere as relaxed as possible. Boredom, isolation and frustration at being incarcerated were all part of the prisoner experience, particularly in the Curragh, which was a rural area and could be extremely cold, damp and windswept in the autumn and winter. The Irish military authorities tried their best to stifle any major issues by exercising common sense when dealing with parole and other freedoms offered to the internees. Moreover, if the internees could be kept relatively contented, this would lessen the chances of an incident, which would in turn reduce the need for any diplomatic interventions by any of the belligerent countries. K-Lines was transparent in a way in which prisoner of war camps simply were not: the men had direct and unsupervised access to their diplomatic representatives, who also visited the camp on a regular basis, their mail was not harshly censored and they could communicate much more readily with the outside world than prisoners of war could.

DOI: 10.1057/9781137446039.0006

These extremely liberal conditions were not the product of a uniquely Irish way of dealing with internment, but were a way to reduce the potential for disorder and dissatisfaction within the belligerent camp. Confining the men to the Curragh as if they were actual prisoners of war was not only contrary to neutral practice, but it was also counter-productive and likely to cause tension between the internees and guards. As Liam Archer of G2 pointed out in October 1940, the best way to deal with them was to try and make them as satisfied with their situation as possible. Furthermore, parole was a method of enforcing control and discipline. As it was a privilege that was granted at the discretion of the camp commandant, it effectively gave the internees something to lose if they misbehaved. On several occasions during the war, parole was suspended, usually after escape attempts, or when there had been a disturbance between the internees. In each of these cases, the trouble subsided when parole privileges were removed and the men were faced with the prospect of being held behind the wire with no hope of relieving the monotony of confinement. Thus when past writers and historians have marvelled at the novelty of the parole system, or mocked the de Valera government for allowing it, they have missed the point entirely.

At the same time, Dublin became involved in the day-to-day lives of prisoners of war as a result of the sending of parcels and packages from Ireland. The very long delay in establishing a free parcel service illustrates that the government was unprepared to deal with the more mundane problems of the war. The criticisms that Rynne and Boland levelled at the Irish Red Cross could also be applied to the government itself. It should have been obvious that being so close to the war zone, and with the tens of thousands of Eire citizens in the British armed forces, there would be a demand for a parcel service, and the lack of one caused unnecessary distress for those who had family members or friends in camps. Boland finally realised that this was not a tenable position: as he wrote in 1943, it was patently ridiculous that an Irish citizen could not obtain the necessary information at their local post office. He told Rynne that he knew of

> a recent case in which, when an Irish citizen who wanted to send something to an Italian internee on the Isle of Man consulted a Post Office, the Post Office assistant looked scandalised as if she had become aware of a plot against the safety of the State, and advised the enquirer to consult this Department to find out "whether it would be allowed".[139]

DOI: 10.1057/9781137446039.0006

His own department, along with several others, were just as negligent as the post office official whom he ridiculed.

Notes

1   M. Mazower (1998) *Dark Continent: Europe's Twentieth Century* (London: Penguin Books), p. 178.
2   L. Rees (2008) *Their Darkest Hour* (London: Ebury Press), p. 81.
3   N. Ferguson (1999) *The Pity of War* (London: Penguin Books), p. 371.
4   E. O'Halpin (2003) *MI5 and Ireland, 1939–1945: The Official History.* (Dublin: Irish Academic Press), p. 103.
5   O'Halpin, *MI5 and Ireland*, p. 103.
6   Girvin, *The Emergency*, p. 83.
7   Irish Military Archives, C229A, Lillis to McNally, 24 August 1940.
8   Irish Military Archives, S/231, O'hAodh to O/C Southern Command, 28 August 1940.
9   Irish Military Archives, S/231, Department of Defence Conference, 13 September 1940.
10 Irish Military Archives, 3/42633, Part I, memo for the Cabinet Committee on Emergency Problem, 18 October 1940.
11 Irish Military Archives, C229A, letter from Liam O'hAodh, 17 December 1940.
12 Irish Military Archives, PM 633/733, 'History of Eire's Belligerent Camps'.
13 Irish Military Archives, S/231, McNally to O'hAodh, 12 September 1940.
14 Irish Military Archives, S/231, Department of Defence Conference, 13 September 1940.
15 Irish Military Archives, S/231, Boland to Archer, 5 September 1940.
16 Irish Military Archives, S/231, Archer to O'hAodh, 6 September 1940.
17 Irish Military Archives, PM633, McNally to O'hAodh, 30 January 1941.
18 Irish Military Archives, C229A, letter from Whelan, 13 June 1941.
19 Irish Military Archives, C229A, Thompson to Adjutant-General, 28 November 1941.
20 Irish Military Archives, PM 633, 'Conference at the Department of Defence on 20th November, 1940, relative to the Conditions of Detention of Interned Members of the Belligerent Armed Forces'.
21 Irish Military Archives, 3/42633, Pt I, 'Extract from British Air Ministry Orders', 15 February 1940.
22 Irish Military Archives, PM 633, 'Conference at the Department of Defence on 20th November, 1940, relative to the Conditions of Detention of Interned Members of the Belligerent Armed Forces'.

DOI: 10.1057/9781137446039.0006

23   Irish Military Archives, PM 733P.
24   Irish Military Archives, PM 733P, 'Discussion in the Taoiseach's office on 23 February 1942'.
25   Irish Military Archives, C229A, report from McNally, 27 November 1940.
26   Irish Military Archives, PM 733P, 'Weekly Report – British and German military internees', 26 March 1941.
27   Irish Military Archives, PM 633, 'Internment – 'B' and 'G' Internment camps, Curragh', McNally to O'hAodh, 28 January 1941.
28   Irish Military Archives PM 733P, 'Weekly Report – British and German military internees', 26 March 1941.
29   Irish Military Archives, PM 633, letter from Provost Marshall to Adjutant-General, February 1941.
30   Irish Military Archives, PM 633, 'Internment – 'B' and 'G' Internment camps, Curragh', McNally to O'hAodh, 28 January 1941.
31   Irish Military Archives, PM633, Report from Provost Marshal to Adjutant-General, May 1941.
32   Irish Military Archives, PM633, letter from Whelan to O'hAodh, 27 February 1941.
33   Irish Military Archives, S/231, 'Discussion at Department of External Affairs on 12 June, 1941'.
34   Tanner, *Refuge from the Reich*, p. 141.
35   Ibid., p. 142.
36   Ibid., p. 148.
37   Ibid., p. 143.
38   J. Nichol and T. Rennell (2003) *The Last Escape: The Untold Story of Allied Prisoners of War in Germany, 1944–45* (London: Penguin), p. 160.
39   M. Hastings (2004) *Armageddon: The Battle for Germany 1944–45* (London: Macmillan), p. 449.
40   National Archives of Ireland, DFA 241/126, letter from Boland, 12 December 1939.
41   National Archives of Ireland, DFA 241/126, letter from Rynne, 18 August 1941.
42   National Archives of Ireland, 241/126, letter from Boland, 17 July 1942.
43   National Archives of Ireland, DFA 369/3, O'Briain to Walshe 17 June 1943.
44   National Archives of Ireland, DFA 369/3, letter from British Red Cross, 1 June 1944.
45   National Archives of Ireland, DFA 369/3, letter from Nolan to Cremin, 18 August 1944.
46   National Archives of Ireland, DFA 369/3, note by Boland 12 August 1943.
47   J. Harte and S. Meara (2007) *To the Limits of Endurance: One Irishman's War* (Dublin: Liberties Press), p. 191.
48   National Archives of Ireland, DFA 241/126, letter from N MacNamara, 21 April 1941.

DOI: 10.1057/9781137446039.0006

49 National Archives of Ireland, DFA 241/126, letter from Irish Red Cross, 9 September 1942.

50 National Archives of Ireland, DFA 243/750, Hankinson to Boland, 23 June 1942.

51 Gilles, *Barbed Wire University*, p. 252.

52 National Archives of Ireland, DFA 241/126, notes of a meeting between Rynne, Cremins and Purcell, 6 January 1941.

53 National Archives of Ireland, DFA 241/126, Boland to Rynne, 14 January 1941.

54 National Archives of Ireland, DFA 369/3, memo by Boland, 17 February 1943.

55 National Archives of Ireland, DFA 369/3, Rynne to Cremins, 10 March 1943.

56 *The Kerryman*, 'Englishman honours war effort of Cloghane native', 20 August 2014.

57 National Archives of Ireland, DFA 369/3, Posts and Telegraphs to External Affairs, 15 February 1943.

58 National Archives of Ireland, DFA 369/3, note 18 February 1943.

59 M. Hastings (2007) *Nemesis: The Battle for Japan, 1944–45* (London: Harper Perennial), p. 381.

60 National Archives of Ireland, DFA 369/3, 'Prisoners of War post', no date.

61 National Archives of Ireland, DFA 369/3, MacMahon to Posts and Telegraphs, no date.

62 National Archives of Ireland, DFA 369/3, 16 February 1943.

63 National Archives of Ireland, DFA 369/3, note by Boland, 17 February 1943.

64 National Archives of Ireland, DFA 369/3, note by Rynne 19 February 1943.

65 National Archives of Ireland, DFA 369/3, note by Rynne 23 February 1943.

66 National Archives of Ireland, DFA 369/3, note by Rynne 10 March 1943.

67 National Archives of Ireland, DFA 369/3, 'Interdepartmental conference re Correspondence for Prisoners of War and Civilians interned abroad – 3 June 1943.'

68 Irish Military Archives, 3/32633, Bryan to Adjutant General, 10 July 1941.

69 Irish Military Archives, C229, Department of Defence Meeting, 10 January 1944.

70 Irish Military Archives, PM 633, letter from MacMahon to Robinson, 28 April 1941.

71 Irish Military Archives, C229A, letter from Mackey, 6 November 1940.

72 Irish Military Archives, C229A, letter from Mackey, 19 November 1940.

73 Irish Military Archives, PM 633, letter from Cementation Company, no date.

74 Irish Military Archives, 2/68904, Pharmaceutical Division of International Red Cross to Irish Red Cross Society 24 January 1945.

75 Irish Military Archives, 2/68904, Ua Moráin to Irish Red Cross, 12 January 1943.

76 Irish Military Archives, 2/68904, Receipt signed by Quedenfeldt, 23 December 1944.

DOI: 10.1057/9781137446039.0006

77   Irish Military Archives, K14, 'Officers Mess Conditions', 28 January 1941.
78   Irish Military Archives , K14, letter from Ward, 24 February 1942.
79   Irish Military Archives , K14, letter from Gribben, 11 September 1943.
80   Irish Military Archives , S/231, Conference, 1 February 1941.
81   National Archives of Ireland, DFA 241/306, Walshe to Fay, 17 October 1941.
82   National Archives of Ireland, DFA 241/306, Boland to Cashman, 3 December 1941.
83   Irish Military Archives , PM 733P, unsigned and undated memo.
84   Irish Military Archives , PM 733P, Lennon to Provost Marshal, 15 February 1944.
85   Dwyer, *Guests of the State*, p. 154.
86   R. Keefer (2002) *Grounded in Eire: The Story of Two RAF Fliers Interned in Ireland during World War II* (Montreal: McGill-Queen's University Press), p. 220.
87   Irish Military Archives, PM 1312, 2 June 1943.
88   Dwyer, *Guests of the State*, p. 158.
89   Irish Military Archives, PM 1312, Henry to McNally, 11 June 1943.
90   Irish Military Archives, PM 1312, 3 June 1943.
91   Irish Military Archives, PM 1426, Callanan to Adjutant General, 13 April 1944.
92   Irish Military Archives, PM 733P, External Affairs conference, 10 October 1944.
93   Irish Military Archives, PM 733P, Henry to O/C No.1 camp, 20 September 1944.
94   R.M. Douglas (2009) *Architects of the Resurrection: Altirí na hAiséirghe and the fascist 'new order' in Ireland* (Manchester: Manchester University Press), p. 223.
95   O'Halpin, *Spying on Ireland*, p. 172.
96   Irish Military Archives, C229, Kuntze and Bielecke to camp commandant, 9 July 1945.
97   Irish Military Archives, PM 733P, Quedenfeld to Camp Commandant, 2 January 1945.
98   Irish Military Archives, PM 633/733, 'History of Eire's Belligerent Camps', no date.
99   Irish Military Archives, C229, McNally to Adjutant-General, 9 February 1944.
100   Irish Military Archives, C229, McNally to Adjutant-General, 24 April 1944.
101   Irish Military Archives, C229, Adjutant-General, 9 February 1944.
102   Irish Military Archives, C229, 'Notes of a meeting held in the office of the Minister for Defence on Monday January 10th, 1944'.
103   Kennedy & Laing, *The Irish Defence Forces*, p. 306.
104   Dwyer, *Guests of the State*, p. 212.

DOI: 10.1057/9781137446039.0006

105 Ibid., p. 197.

106 Irish Military Archives, C229, letter from McAllister, undated.

107 Irish Military Archives, C229, letter from Guiney to O/C Curragh, 3 January 1945.

108 I. Kershaw (2000) *Hitler 1936 – 1945: Nemesis*. (London: Allen Lane the Penguin Press), p. 746.

109 Irish Military Archives, CP 1759, letter from O'Neill to O/C No.1 camp, 23 May 1945.

110 Irish Military Archives, CP 1759, letter from Costello to Adjutant-General, 22 May 1945.

111 Kennedy, *Guarding Neutral Ireland*, p. 296.

112 Dwyer, *Guests of the State*, p. 223.

113 National Archives of Ireland, DFA 241/306, Boland to Cashman, 3 December 1941.

114 National Archives of Ireland, DFA 241/309, Ua Moráin to Boland, 9 April 1943.

115 Irish Military Archives, C229, 'Notes of a meeting held in the office of the Minister for Defence on Monday January 10th, 1944'.

116 Irish Military Archives, C229, Gaffney to Command Adjutant, 11 August 1944.

117 Dwyer, *Guests of the State*, p. 211.

118 Irish Military Archives, PM 1721, 2 March 1945.

119 Ibid.

120 Dwyer, *Guests of the State*, p. 195.

121 S. Scheipers (2010) *Prisoners in War* (Oxford: Oxford University Press), p. 5.

122 J. Custodis (2011) 'Exploiting the Enemy in the Orkneys: The Employment of Italian Prisoners of War on the Scapa Flow Barriers during the Second World War' *Journal of Scottish Historical Studies*, 31, 1, 75.

123 B. Girvin and G. Roberts (2000) *Ireland in the Second World War: Politics, Society and Remembrance* (Dublin: Four Courts Press), p. 121–22.

124 Dwyer, *Guests of the State*, p. 220.

125 National Archives of Ireland, DFA 241/309, Gaffney and Murphy to Chief Superintendent, 24 April 1943.

126 Irish Military Archives, C229, 'Notes of a meeting held in the office of the Minister for Defence on Monday January 10th, 1944'.

127 Irish Military Archives, CP 1737, Collins-Powell to Provost Marshal, 24 April 1945.

128 National Archives of Ireland, DFA 241/309, Boland to MacMahon, 6 October 1943.

129 National Archives of Ireland, DFA 241/309, Rynne to Assistant Secretary, 4 May 1942.

130 *Daily Telegraph*, 'Our Troops in Switzerland: Fighting Boredom in Camp', 1 March 1944.

DOI: 10.1057/9781137446039.0006

131   National Archives of Ireland, DFA 241/309, Ua Moráin to Walshe, 20 June 1944.
132   Irish Military Archives, CP 1737, Collins-Powell to Provost Marshal, 24 April 1945.
133   Irish Military Archives, PM 1721, 2 March 1945.
134   Dwyer, *Guests of the State*, p. 200.
135   Irish Military Archives, CP 1737, Collins-Powell to Provost Marshal, 24 April 1945.
136   Irish Military Archives, CP 1737, Collins-Powell to Provost Marshal, 23 April 1945.
137   Irish Military Archives, C229, Guiney to Provost Marshal, 13 July 1944.
138   National Archives of Ireland, DFA 241/309, Boland to Ferguson, 15 May 1945.
139   National Archives of Ireland, DFA 369/3, Boland to Rynne, 4 March 1943.

DOI: 10.1057/9781137446039.0006

4
Breaking Out and Breaking In: Escape

Abstract: *Fears of international repercussions meant that the Irish government took great care to ensure that no military internees died while in its military custody, and that punishments for escape attempts were extremely lenient, particularly in contrast to Switzerland. At the same time, the issue of German prisoners of war escaping from camps in Northern Ireland into neutral Eire was deemed to be of such high importance that the government decided to abandon international law entirely, and secretly intercept and expel escapers under Irish legislation designed to restrict the entry of illegal aliens. This represented a fundamental breach of neutrality and, as this chapter shows, highlights again that the de Valera government always chose to preserve relations with the Allies rather than strictly enforce international guidelines on neutrality.*

Keywords: aliens; expulsion; firearms; Northern Ireland; Royal Ulster Constabulary

Kelly, Bernard. *Military Internees, Prisoners of War and the Irish State during the Second World War.* Basingstoke: Palgrave Macmillan, 2015. DOI: 10.1057/9781137446039.0007.

Escape of belligerent internees and prisoners of war was a major preoc-
cupation for the de Valera government during the Emergency. While the
military internees were held in Ireland, 11 Allied and one German successfully broke out of the Curragh; two of these men were polite enough to
write letters of thanks and apologies to the Irish army authorities. In
his letter, Pilot Officer Cowper described his regret for 'all the trouble I
may have caused by my escape'.[1] The single German was recaptured and
handed to the British authorities. Escape attempts from K-Lines emphasised the differences between belligerent internees and prisoners of war.
Although the PA were armed, carried live ammunition and were authorised to use it, they were discouraged from firing on escaping internees.
This was partly because there was no legal precedent that gave Ireland
the authority to fire on internees, but also because Dublin was eager to
avoid the severe ramifications of the death of an internee at the hands
of the Irish army. In addition, the determination of some internees to
break out also highlighted the frustration of the Department of Defence
with how the camp was run, and McNally in particular reported that
the need to maintain a good relationship with the internees hampered
precautions against escape. This same consideration did not exist in the
IRA camp, where PAs were also authorised to use firearms against the
inmates, resulting in the death of one inmate in December 1940.

However, another pressing issue confronting the government was prisoners of war attempting to get *into* Eire. In late 1944, over 10,000 German
prisoners of war were transferred to Northern Ireland, to relieve severe
overcrowding in camps in Britain. Under international law, prisoners
of war who reached neutral territory could, technically, be immune
from detention, as arresting and detaining them could be interpreted
as continuing their initial captivity. The spectre of German prisoners
of war breaking out of Northern Ireland and seeking refuge in Eire was
not one welcomed by the de Valera government. The large numbers of
Germans already interned, who were dependant on Irish funds as the
German Legation was in deep financial difficulty, already stretched Irish
resources to the limit. Quite apart from that, the diplomatic impact
would have been catastrophic. There was simply no way that the British
or US governments would acquiesce to German prisoners of war being
left at large in Eire, given that the continuing presence of official Axis
Legations in Dublin had already been a point of contention. In addition,
in September 1944 de Valera refused an Allied demand that Ireland
deny Axis war criminals entry to the country. In order to pre-empt the

DOI: 10.1057/9781137446039.0007

problem, the government exploited the lack of precise international regulation governing escaping prisoners of war and decided to establish a cordon around the border with Northern Ireland to intercept any would-be German escapers before they reached the Irish interior. Any that managed to slip through would be arrested and expelled under Irish law, regardless of their legal status vis-à-vis the Hague and Geneva conventions or practices followed in other neutral countries.

The question of escape was on the government's agenda as soon as the first belligerent personnel were interned in the Curragh. As previously mentioned, Colonel Thomas McNally was extremely wary of the first German internees, viewing them as men who were determined to flee at the first opportunity. The tight security, which characterised life in K-Lines during the first few weeks, was, in his view, fully justified by the risk that the internees would seek to break out. He reported that Mollenhauer had told him openly of his intention to escape and asked the Adjutant-General to confirm 'the amount of force which I may employ to prevent such escape'.[2] The situation became more complex after the first British pilot, Mayhew, was interned in September 1940. Despite McNally's suspicions regarding the Germans, it was the Allied internees who were far more likely to attempt to escape. The border with Northern Ireland was less than 100 miles away from the Curragh, and the area surrounding the camp contained many people who were sympathetic to the Allied cause. The quandary faced by the government, and by the Irish military, was how to effectively guard the internees while also ensuring that the amount of force used did not provoke a complaint from the belligerent states. One measure that was taken swiftly was that the use of weapons was restricted. Draft instructions drawn up for McNally in December 1940 make it clear that while an escort was to stay with the internees when they were on parole, deadly force was strongly discouraged:

> If the circumstances should arise in which it became necessary to choose between the use of firearms and allowing an internee on parole to escape, the latter course should be followed.[3]

It is clear that this decision came directly from de Valera himself, and caused some difficulty in the early days of Mayhew's internment. As he was initially refused permission by London to sign out on parole, McNally was willing to allow him to leave his compound if followed by an armed escort. However, the instruction to allow Mayhew to escape rather than firing at him meant that the provision of the armed escort was pointless. The decision not to use weapons differed from the Swedish practice: internees being transferred from one camp to another by the Swedish authorities were warned that 'if they attempt to escape they may be shot'.[4]

Although discouraged to use their rifles, the PAs at K-Lines were not expressly forbidden to do so: the official duties laid down for the camp sentries stated, somewhat vaguely, that they could 'use such force as may be necessary to prevent the escape or rescue of Internees'.[5] Instructions to the camp Guard were clearer, stating that they were permitted to open fire to 'prevent the rescue or the attempted rescue of the Internees', or to prevent the destruction of property. In these limited circumstances, guards could fire without warning. What was missing from the instructions, however, was the authorisation to fire on internees effecting their own escape, as distinct from being rescued from outside the camp.[6] The instructions handed to sentinels at No.4 camp at Gormanstown were much clearer: sentinels were to fire into the air only to raise the alarm in the case of an escape.[7] This differed from the standing orders at the IRA camp, which declared that military police could, without prior warning, fire live ammunition to prevent either escape or rescue.[8] Furthermore, Emergency Powers Order no.28 stated quite clearly that the Defence Forces could 'use such force (including the use of firearms) as may be reasonably necessary to prevent the escape or rescue' of republican internees or convicted prisoners.[9]

On 20 January 1941, the British internees disabled the electrical systems at K-Lines, scaled the wire and several escaped into the night, although all were quickly recaptured. Reporting to the Quartermaster General, McNally asked for more lights surrounding the camp, and sarcastically highlighted the particular difficulties he faced:

> I am perfectly satisfied that the British and German Internees are aware of the fact that we cannot fire on them and that their attempts to escape, therefore, can be made without fear of being killed or maimed. In this connection I might mention that I have personally observed a Curragh sheep making its way through the barbed wire defences in No.1 Internment camp. It took it exactly one minute to do so.[10]

McNally raised further concerns about the ambiguous position of the camp guards following a large break out on the night of 25 June 1941. Nine Allied internees overpowered the PAs on duty, six of which eventually made it to Northern Ireland,[11] and McNally requested that extra guards be drafted into the camp. He was particularly anxious about the options open to the PAs when breakouts occurred:

> A point which is causing me great concern is the overpowering of the Military Police personnel. As you are aware only the barest minimum is on duty at any one time and their duties are mainly of an observational nature. They could not hope to resist a massed attack from the Internees who considerably outnumber them. In this connection sentries are practically useless except to give an alarm as they cannot fire on the Internees, and I know the Internees took this into consideration when planning their escape.[12]

Despite the prohibition, two guards fired a total of five shots at or over the internees during the escape.[13] It should be noted that not all the PAs at K-Lines were armed. Only sentries who manned the observation posts actually carried their rifles and they were supposed to keep watch on the wire perimeter, rather than the internees themselves.[14] Members of the camp Guard, fifteen men and an NCO, left their rifles in the Guard Room.[15] The remaining PAs and soldiers carried batons and some officers carried revolvers. An official military inquiry into the June 1941 escape showed the growing contradiction between the duty of Defence to ensure the internees did not escape and the stated desire of External Affairs that this be achieved with minimum force, while allowing the internees the maximum amount of freedom. Extra barriers were not erected around K-Lines because of 'the continuous objection of the Internees to be made even appear as prisoners'. This, combined with the 'question of preserving harmonious relations and the fostering of goodwill' meant that the camp's perimeter was not reinforced. This placed McNally in a very difficult position, as the enquiry confirmed when it absolved him of blame for the escape. The main problem identified by the enquiry was that

> While the utmost courtesy and civility must be extended to the Internees, yet they must be prevented from escaping. The working out in practice of these two rather opposed points of view is likely to lead to other incidents similar to the one the Court just investigated.[16]

The successful escape led directly to a letter of protest from Hempel, who claimed in July that Ireland was in breach of international law by not guarding the internees closely enough.[17] As a possible defence to this, Rynne suggested that Hempel be informed of the practical difficulties of holding the British internees: they could blend in with the local population because they spoke English, British forces were close by in Ulster and

DOI: 10.1057/9781137446039.0007

because they were not actually 'prisoners of war, we are unwilling to fire upon [them] (a reluctance which benefits the German internees also)'.[18]

In January 1942, a British internee attempted to escape by scaling the wire while his comrade distracted the guards; when confronted by PAs with rifles, his fellow internee shouted that they were under orders not to fire and urged him to run. This development particularly troubled McNally, who felt that the camp guards were now in an 'impossible position' because the internees had 'definitely and for all time established that our police and sentries cannot shoot them when attempting to escape'. His frustration seeped through his letter to the Adjutant-General, which concluded by suggesting that 'It might be a convenient time to consider whether or not a military camp of this nature is the most suitable place for the internment of belligerents'.[19] It is difficult not to have some sympathy for McNally at this point. Under constant pressure from External Affairs to adopt as liberal an attitude as possible towards internees, he was still expected to prevent them from escaping but was unable to offer strong resistance when they inevitably tried. Shortly afterwards, Peadar MacMahon, secretary of the Department of Defence, questioned the prohibition on the use of firearms in a letter to External Affairs. He pointed out that international law seemed to allow force to be used on internees and then asked if Ireland was not actually breaching international law by not using all means to prevent internees escaping,[20] echoing Hempel's remarks of July 1941.

The situation came to a head on the night of 7 February 1942 when the entire Allied camp attempted to break out. The getaway was thwarted by PAs, who made liberal use of their batons, and also fired shots over the heads of the escapers. In the days afterwards both Maffey and de Valera became involved, and Maffey suggested that the guards should not have firearms at all, as 'the temptation to fire on the internees if they tried to escape might be too strong'.[21] In this, Maffey had a point: despite the repeated reminders, shots were fired during all the major escape attempts at K-Lines. When he examined the issue, Rynne could find no basis upon which Ireland could justify the use of firearms on escaping internees, despite External Affairs having evidence that Swedish regulations warned internees of the danger of being shot while escaping. He argued that Ireland's main role model, Switzerland, did not sanction a policy of firing on internees. If it happened in Ireland, he wrote, 'it would be almost impossible for us to justify the killing of an internee in the Curragh'.[22] Boland foresaw the diplomatic consequences, telling the

DOI: 10.1057/9781137446039.0007

Department of Defence that 'a very difficult situation would be created if a British internee was shot trying to escape, particularly if he were killed'.[23]

No Axis or Allied personnel died while in the custody of the Irish military, during escapes or otherwise, and figures have not yet been discovered which would allow a comparison with other European neutrals. The government did its very best to ensure that military internees received the best standard of medical attention and they had access to the Curragh military facilities. If they could not be treated in Kildare, they were given travel vouchers to travel to Dublin and, if needed, an interpreter was sent with them.[24] In addition, arrangements were made to have emergency supplies of blood available for transfusion in the event that belligerent pilots were injured in crashes on Irish territory.[25] While none died in captivity, many belligerent personnel died on Irish territory, usually when their aircraft crashed. One hundred and fifty nine British, 11 American and 24 Germans died after crashing on Irish territory, with a further 12 British pilots listed as missing.[26] In addition, four German sailors died after being rescued by the *Kerlogue*.

The aftermath of the attempted February 1942 escape illustrated an interesting difference between the Irish and Swiss approaches to their respective military internees and, despite the fact the External Affairs constantly looked to Switzerland as a model, this was one instance in which their policies diverged completely. As previously noted, the Swiss government declined in 1940 to extend the provisions of the 1929 Geneva Convention to belligerent internees, while the Irish government was happy to do so. The Convention stipulated that if prisoners were to be punished for escape attempts, then any punishment should not exceed 30 days and that they must not be transferred to another institution to serve it. Escapes in K-Lines usually only resulted in partial or temporary loss of parole or, if outside assistance was suspected, a brief stoppage and more intensive search of incoming mail. As Ireland adhered to the Convention, none of these punishments contradicted the international standard. Following the June 1941 breakout, de Valera made a point of reminding Defence that no punishments were to surpass the thirty day limit set out in 1929 and he hoped that the internees would not be penalised at all.[27] The Swiss, on the other hand, handed down prison sentences of between three and six months to escapers and sometimes transferred them to the disciplinary camp at Wauwilermoos, where American internees reported filthy conditions, overcrowding, strict

DOI: 10.1057/9781137446039.0007

security, poor food[28] and where prisoners were not allowed to receive Red Cross parcels.[29] Swiss prosecutors defended this practice by claiming that punishment of 30 days was not sufficient to stop escape attempts and that if Switzerland could not effectively detain internees, it might damage their neutrality.[30]

By way of contrast, when it was suggested that some of the British internees might be charged with assault for their part in the scuffles on the night of 7 February, Michael Rynne noted that as Ireland had decided to adopt the 1929 rules as the basis of its internment policy, the internees in question could not be brought before a military or a civilian court for their actions during an escape attempt. Instead, they could be dealt with by disciplinary action within the camp,[31] and as a result their parole privileges were temporarily curtailed. The Swiss refusal to implement the Convention meant that escapers were sentenced under Swiss law, meaning that belligerent internees were often given harsher treatment than prisoners of war in belligerent countries who were caught escaping.

The question of what actually constituted an escape was brought into question during the June 1941 breakout, when two British internees returning from parole distracted the guards at the gate while their comrades rushed out of the camp. A subsequent military enquiry ruled that both internees had broken their parole by assisting an escape[32] and External Affairs suggested that they would be willing to ask the British authorities to return the men,[33] although they eventually decided against it. However, when Roland Wolfe, who had been interned at the end of November 1941, played a simple but clever sleight-of-hand with his parole privileges to escape the camp, the question was raised again. On 13 December 1941, he signed out on parole for the night. However, he pretended to forget something and signed back into the camp to retrieve it, walking back to his room. After a few minutes, he returned to the gate, where the PA on duty then allowed him out without signing a new parole form. He then spent the night in Dublin before presenting himself at his base in Derry the next day. When the matter was investigated, the camp guards claimed that Wolfe had not returned to his room but had simply absconded, but one of Wolfe's colleagues confirmed his story.[34] Although he had technically not been on parole when he left the camp, his ruse threatened to undermine the liberal manner in which the camp was run. All internees signed undertakings not to escape, or make preparations to escape, while out on parole, but Wolfe's use of it to flee was also considered to be out of order. If he had been allowed to go free, then the parole

DOI: 10.1057/9781137446039.0007

system would undoubtedly have been tightened up considerably, as other internees would certainly have tried variations of Wolfe's scheme. Parole was one of the mechanisms which maintained the camp's relative harmony; closely confining the men could conceivably led to increased tensions and possible incidents. Maffey suggested that Wolfe be returned, to avoid the Irish authorities having to clamp down on the internees, which he was a few days later. It should be noted that David Gray, despite his well-known opposition to Irish neutrality, agreed with Maffey and supported the decision to return Wolfe to detention.[35] Subsequently, all escape attempts were formulated from inside the wire. They included a foiled tunnel from K-Lines and another at Gormanstown,[36] which was discovered personally by the camp commander, Captain T.J. Ringrose. The tunnel was closely monitored by the camp authorities, who even created a diagram of its probable route,[37] and it was shut down shortly before the last Allied internees were released in June 1944.

The arrival of thousands of German prisoners of war in Northern Ireland in January 1945 surprised both the Belfast and Dublin governments. The Unionist administration was not consulted before the decision was made and was informed only in early December 1944 that approximately 12,400 German prisoners were going to be sent,[38] and would be shipped between 8 and 20 January.[39] Stormont Minister for Home Affairs Edmund Warnock wrote that the Prime Minister of Northern Ireland, Sir Basil Brooke, was opposed to the plan, but that his government would cooperate if requested.[40] Belfast also warned about the danger of 'escapes to Eire and the likelihood of these men finding some sympathy with certain elements in our midst,'[41] in other words the IRA and the nationalist population. Likewise, when Maffey told Dublin of the decision on 6 January, Joseph Walshe protested strongly, telling Maffey that 'if it was absolutely necessary to send prisoners to the Six Counties, his authorities should take the greatest care to prevent them from escaping into our area.'[42] Despite the obvious reluctance of the Belfast administration as well as the objections from Dublin, the British government had little choice but to send prisoners to Northern Ireland. By 1943, with vast numbers of Italians in camps all over Britain and the Dominions, and an ever-growing number of Germans also being captured, the British government began to run out of space.[43] Prisoner numbers also surged once the Allied forces landed at Normandy and began to advance through France. Prisoners and internees were shipped to Canada from 1940 onwards, and South Africa also hosted German

DOI: 10.1057/9781137446039.0007

prisoners of war, despite the precarious political and security situation there.[44] Northern Ireland was the last empty area available to the British and it had the added advantage that it was close by.

The Germans in Northern Ireland were held in six wired camps that had previously housed American troops and, unlike the rest of the UK, would not be available for employment.[45] There was also to be a hospital for the prisoners at Orangefield, near Belfast, that would be staffed and run by German doctors and nurses overseen by British officials.[46] Like K-Lines, the camp guards were armed and the government in London was not keen to see prisoners being killed. The Royal Ulster Constabulary (RUC) was advised that 'armed guards have definite instructions to shoot to kill in the event of an attempted prisoner-of-war escape'. However, the Home Office in London pointed out that they would 'prefer to be relieved of any possible embarrassment that might ensue from the questions which would almost inevitably arise if an armed member of the Royal Ulster Constabulary did in fact shoot and killed [sic] an escaping German prisoner-of-war'. The Home Office instead asked that the RUC use their discretion about the use of live ammunition, particularly if faced with armed prisoners.[47] One German prisoner in Northern Ireland was killed during an escape attempt, shot by a sentry at Monrush camp in March 1945.[48]

Some sections of the Northern Irish press and public reacted badly to the news that German prisoners were soon to arrive. While the *Belfast News Letter* assured its readers that the Germans were not hardcore Nazis and that all roads to Eire were under heavy guard,[49] the *Daily Mail* headline thundered dramatically that there was a 'Spate of Nazis for N.Ireland'.[50] A Derry business owner wrote to John Maynard Sinclair, the acting prime minister in Belfast, asking him not to send any prisoners to the province, warning that 'it would be very easy for the Germans if they escaped to get over the border and they would be very well received by the Free Staters'.[51] In the rest of the UK the fear of fifth columnists was synchronised with the course of the war, falling away after peaking in mid-1940, but in Northern Ireland the spectre of internal enemies never dissipated. The unionist government had deep misgivings about the loyalty of the Catholic/nationalist minority within the six counties and from Belfast's perspective the coming of thousands of German prisoners, combined with the ever-present threat of the IRA, was not an appealing prospect. The cross-border reach of the IRA before stern action was taken against it by Dublin and Belfast was demonstrated by the fact that

DOI: 10.1057/9781137446039.0007

some of the ammunition stolen by republicans from the Magazine Fort raid in Dublin during December 1939 was used in attacks in Northern Ireland.[52]

The influx of Germans could scarcely have come at a worse time for the Dublin government. Twice in 1944 there had been tense diplomatic stand-offs between Ireland and the Allies: in February 1944 the American Note threatened to plunge Irish-US relations into crisis, and in September the Allies requested an assurance the Ireland would not grant asylum to any Axis war criminals.

Both of these requests were viewed in Dublin as unacceptable attempts to limit Irish sovereignty and de Valera inevitably refused to grant either, leading to much negative publicity in Allied countries. Upon hearing of the impending arrival of German prisoners, Michael Rynne was tasked with investigating the legal aspects of the situation, and where Eire stood in relation to escaped prisoners of war. He discovered that, despite the firm guidelines set out in the 1907 Hague Convention, there was actually no consensus amongst legal scholars. The language of the convention seemed to offer little room for manoeuvre: 'A neutral Power which receives escaped prisoners of war shall leave them at liberty. If it allows them to remain in its territory it may assign them a place of residence.'[53] Of particular interest was Britain's official attitude to escaped prisoners of war. In 1907, as one of the main signatories, London proposed an amendment which stated that 'Prisoners who, having escaped from the territory of a belligerent which held them (or from enemy territory occupied by a belligerent) arrive in a neutral country shall be free.'[54] However, in the intervening years, this opinion had been modified. For instance, the British manual of military law (which had been largely adopted by the Irish Defence Forces) stated that:

> Prisoners of war who succeed in escaping into neutral territory regain their liberty, but they cannot claim to remain there. It rests with the neutral State whether it will grant or refuse them admission, and in the latter case whether or not it will allow them to remain on its territory. If they are permitted to remain the neutral State may compel them to make their residence in a specified locality.[55]

Maffey contradicted this when he met Walshe to discuss the matter in January 1945, he asked that the Dublin government hand any escapers back to the British authorities, which Walshe refused to guarantee.[56] European models were of little use to Ireland either. Switzerland arranged

DOI: 10.1057/9781137446039.0007

to hand over escaping British prisoners of war who crossed its frontiers to the advancing Allied armies, while Swedish regulations simply stated that while escapers were not 'internable' they were to be turned over to the local authorities.[57]

Rynne's recommendations eventually chose a middle way between the two extremes of interning escapers or leaving them at liberty. Noting that a neutral country could deny escaping prisoners entry if they wished, Rynne suggested the creation of a special 'zone of control' along the border with Northern Ireland, extending approximately 35 miles into Eire territory. German prisoners who were caught within this zone were considered to still be in the act of escaping and could therefore be turned back. De Valera himself approved this idea on 13 January 1945.[58] The fate of those who managed to evade the Gardaí and pass through the zone remained unresolved. Although Walshe suggested to Maffey that they would be interned,[59] and Colonel Dan Bryan of G2 thought that they should be 'under some form of restraint,'[60] it was far from clear where they would be accommodated. Bryan was of the opinion that they could only be held in the German internment camp in the Curragh, but was unaware if there was actually space there.[61] The key to the Irish strategy was to prevent escapers getting into the interior of Eire but, as Rynne noted, the Gardaí would not be able to contain a mass breakout from Northern Ireland.[62]

Unlike the internment of the belligerent airmen and sailors, Dublin did not rely on emergency law to halt prisoners of war entering Eire. Instead, the instructions issued by the Gardaí on 18 January cited the Aliens Act of 1935.[63] The act gave the Minister for Justice the power to prevent aliens from entering the country, as well as the power to compel them to stay in 'particular places or districts' in Ireland.[64] Presumably, if any prisoners of war managed to slip through the control zone, the latter clause would have been used to detain and control them, but it did not specify that they had to be kept within one camp. Gardaí were to ascertain whether any Germans caught in this area had the correct documentation allowing them to cross the border and, if they did not, they were to be 'escorted without delay to the Border and put across into Northern Ireland'. Escapers would not, of course, have the correct permits or a passport meaning that the government could expel them under Irish law.

Not using emergency legislation had two other advantages for the de Valera government. As Rynne admitted in January 1946, Dublin was technically supposed to allow escaping prisoners of war attempt to rejoin their own forces,[65] as Switzerland did. Any Emergency Powers Order which attempted to expel escapers from Eire would draw attention to the fact that the government had not even attempted to conform to the 1907 Convention. It could also be questioned in the Dáil, as the order to dismiss deserters from the Irish Defence Forces was in October 1945. In addition, as has previously been illustrated, the government was closely questioned by independent TD Oliver Flanagan regarding releases of Allied aircrew, and there is little doubt that he would have seized upon this issue to further embarrass de Valera. By using the 1935 Aliens Act as the basis for its actions, the government simply bypassed its obligations as a neutral and, instead of regarding escaping Germans as prisoners of war, instead chose to classify them as foreign nationals attempting to make an illegal entry into Eire, almost as if the war was not in progress. The orders issued to the Gardaí make no mention of prisoners at all and instead consistently refer to them as aliens. The use of existing legislation, the convenient classification as aliens and the use of censorship to remove all mention of the escapers in the Irish media, meant that the government could quickly and quietly deal with any escaped prisoners of war and avoid any unpleasant explanations either to the Dáil or to the British government.

The first escapers crossed quickly into Irish territory. Within 48 hours of the decision being made, two German prisoners appeared in Dundalk and handed themselves into the local Garda station. They were part of a group of four who had escaped from a camp in Gilford, county Down, two of whom had been intercepted by the British. As the two which had reached Eire had been apprehended within three miles of the border and were therefore still within the control zone, the Gardaí were given instructions that they should be sent straight back. Having been given a cup of tea and washing facilities, the two men were driven to the border and went 'quite cheerfully' when they were sent back into Northern Ireland.[66] There is no hint in the documents that the RUC had warned the Gardaí about the escapers, and the local police in Dundalk were as surprised as anyone when the two Germans surrendered themselves.

Great secrecy was attached to the plan to prevent prisoners crossing into Eire. In a meeting with Norman Archer of the British Legation, Walshe stressed the need to stop the press publishing the news of escapes,[67] and the official instructions issued to the police emphasised

DOI: 10.1057/9781137446039.0007

that the order was 'strictly confidential'.[68] The Irish censor removed an article in the *Irish Independent* which stated that the two men had made it over the border,[69] and the articles that were allowed to be published were very light on details. The *Daily Express* reported on the recapture of the two men, but made a point of saying that the 'Ulster police are reticent about their capture'.[70] On 11 July 1945 a further two Germans were discovered in Louth. With the war over at that point and the censorship regime dismantled, the press were free to report on the matter. Newspaper accounts suggested that the men had fled from a camp in France, travelling across Britain to reach Northern Ireland, where they then crossed into Eire. However, G2 suspected that they had actually broken out of an English camp and lied about it in an attempt to avoid being returned.[71] They finally admitted the truth, which was that they were both deserters from the German forces, one of whom had fled to Sweden and the other who had surrendered to the Americans in France.[72] None of this helped their case and de Valera personally ordered that they be 'sent across the border' on 10 July.[73]

The manner in which prisoners were returned to Northern Ireland was very specific. Walshe informed Maffey that because of the implications for Irish neutrality, Dublin could not officially return the prisoners to the RUC.[74] This was tantamount to continuing their captivity and aiding Britain to detain them, which would represent a very serious and very public breach of neutrality. Therefore, the Gardaí were specially instructed that they 'will not be formally handed over to the R.U.C'.[75] Likewise, Dan Bryan of G2 suggested that they be simply 'pushed back'.[76] Although considerations surrounding neutrality was given as the overt reason, there was another motive. Because Dublin had a continuing claim on the territory of Northern Ireland, the de Valera government was keen to avoid any public action which would seem to recognise or legitimise the northern Irish state. Therefore, despite the fact that there was a great deal of cross-border cooperation during the war, the Gardaí could not be seen to be publicly collaborating with the RUC, as it could have serious political repercussions. As one senior Garda reported, it was assumed by the population in Louth that the police were officially assisting the RUC in capturing escaped prisoners of war, and the Dundalk branch of the Fianna Fáil party – de Valera's own – raised the issue at one of its meetings.[77] The need for secrecy was paramount if the government was to avoid embarrassment and the façade of neutrality was to be maintained.

DOI: 10.1057/9781137446039.0007

The mass escapes envisaged by the press and feared by the Dublin government never materialised. Despite the *Sunday Pictorial* warning that the IRA was plotting to spring 2,000 Germans from captivity,[78] only 20 Germans escaped from camps in Northern Ireland. Some authors have presented anecdotal evidence of Germans successfully getting across the border,[79] but the documentary evidence shows that only three made it to Eire before the end of the war in Europe, with several more arriving afterwards. For those who arrived during the conflict, all were detained by the police for a short period and then ferried back to the border. The lack of escapes was partly due to the fact that the Germans in Northern Ireland were guarded very tightly, and that their stay was extremely brief: most remained there only until August 1945, when 8,000 of them were shipped back to Britain.[80] By December only 997 were left in Ulster.[81] By this stage the IRA was in no condition, north or south, to attack the camps, regardless of the doom-laden predictions in some newspapers. Internment on both sides of the border had greatly weakened the organisation, which by 1945 was far more focussed on survival than taking the offensive against either Irish state.

While Dublin had to deal with Germans in Northern Ireland for only a short period, more German prisoners of war arrived from an unexpected direction well after the end of the conflict. On 19 January 1946, a small coastal patrol boat containing fifteen German sailors arrived in Kinsale harbour, having escaped from the French naval base at St. Nazaire. They sought out the local Garda station and made contact with a local solicitor, who wrote to External Affairs on their behalf. The Germans requested that they be repatriated to their homes in the British and American occupation zones of Germany; failing that, they wished to be given asylum in Ireland or to travel onwards the Britain, but they refused to be sent back to France.[82] While in Kinsale, they were provided with food at the State's expense, but were also given packages by the local branch of the Red Cross. Their presence generated a number of reactions amongst the population of the coastal town. Many were simply curious, while others were sympathetic enough to send them gifts of food. Relatives of those who had died in the war were understandably hostile to the Germans.[83] Cork, and other areas of Munster, had long traditions of providing recruits for the Royal Navy. However, the sister of a prisoner of war who had been held by the Germans, and well treated by them, invited the sailors to tea at her house.[84] The Department of External Affairs was careful to record and preserve the

DOI: 10.1057/9781137446039.0007

extensive press coverage given to the Germans arrival and the attitude of the local population. Unsurprisingly taken completely unawares by their landing, the government, as always, looked to Rynne to establish their legal position.

Rynne noted immediately that as Germany had surrendered and hostilities had ended, Ireland's neutrality was not a factor. Instead, the Germans could be considered 'ordinary aliens' who had landed without a permit and were therefore liable to expulsion, the same category that had been applied to escaping prisoners of war. However, even in peacetime international relations had to be taken into account. As they had escaped from French custody, Rynne worried that 'A serious diplomatic incident might be created with France, or the Allies generally' if the men were permitted to remain in Ireland. Even more worryingly, if they were allowed to stay, this would set a precedent and Dublin then ran the risk of becoming 'a refuge for all the displaced persons of Europe with the means of landing unexpectedly here'. His recommendation was the same as the issue of prisoners from Northern Ireland: to use the Aliens Act to expel them and, in this case, to arrange with the French authorities to take them back into custody.[85]

After consultations with the French Legation in Dublin, the government followed Rynne's suggestion to the letter, and a French corvette was sent to Cobh on 7 February to take the sailors back into custody, and to take possession of the stolen boat. They were transported with a heavy police presence to Cobh and there handed over to the French. The incident sparked a protest from Fine Gael TD Eamon O'Neill, whose wife had been one of the Red Cross officials providing assistance to the sailors. Writing to Walshe in March 1946, he said that he felt 'very sore about the way the Germans had been treated', particularly the manner of the handover to the French. The Germans had not been informed of their destination until the last minute, and were 'packed in a bus with fifteen beefy Guards (the biggest in Cork) who did not treat them too kindly and shoved them roughly down the wharf at Cobh into the French corvette'.[86] Replying a few weeks later, Walshe informed O'Neill that the Germans had been expelled purely on the grounds of controlling illegal immigration. If they had not been, Walshe argued, then Ireland would become 'a happy hunting-ground for every kind of "displaced person" who manages to get here from Europe'.[87] In the Dáil, O'Neill asked de Valera which countries Ireland had extradition treaties with, to which de Valera said that Ireland had none.[88]

DOI: 10.1057/9781137446039.0007

The government set aside extra ammunition to refute O'Neill's arguments in the form of a British decision in 1946 to expel four Polish men who had stowed away on a ship to Scotland and sought asylum. In defending the decision to eject the Poles, the British Home Secretary James Chuter Ede said that 'it is essential that no encouragement should be given to the idea that persons who come to this country illegally will receive preferential treatment'.[89] At the time, the British government was attempting to resettle thousands of Polish veterans of the war in the UK, and was coming under pressure from trade unions not to admit any more.[90] An External Affairs note for de Valera pointed out that Ede's 'statement covers our position as regards the fifteen Germans at Kinsale very accurately and, therefore, the second sentence of Mr Ede's reply might be useful in the event of Deputy O'Neill asking supplementaries'.[91]

Much like the policy towards German escapers from Northern Ireland, there was a large amount of deception surrounding the removal of the German sailors. As Rynne observed, O'Neill's question could not have come at a worse time. At that time, there was no basis in Irish law to extradite a foreign national upon request from abroad. The Extradition Act of 1870 could be used in an emergency, but as it was a pre-independence law which referred to the Irish as 'British subjects', the de Valera government preferred not to use it. 'If it were possible to avoid disclosing the details of this situation to the Dáil, so much the better' wrote Rynne. 'Such a disclosure might have a bad effect abroad, as well as on the deputies.' According to Rynne's advice, the sailors were not technically extradited, as O'Neill had implied; they had been expelled under the Aliens Act and, as they were members of the German forces which had surrendered to the Allies, Ireland had to recognise that the French government 'had a claim to the custody of these men'.[92] In addition, once the arrangements with the French government had been concluded, Frederick Boland telephoned the Department of Justice, warning them about arresting the sailors too early in advance of the French arrival, as that would give their lawyers time to file habeas corpus applications. He was told that the Gardaí had decided to 'postpone the arrest until the last moment'.[93]

Rynne acknowledged in 1948 that any legal action taken by escaped prisoners of war against their expulsion by Dublin would be difficult to defend against. Putting together a hypothetical court case brought by an escaped prisoner of war against the Irish state, he argued that even if the Court found against the applicant,

DOI: 10.1057/9781137446039.0007

despite this Department's assurances that Ireland has overtly assumed all the obligations of the Hague Conventions, and, in particular, those deriving from Convention No. V of 1907 concerning the rights and duties of neutral powers in case of war on land, it is scarcely conceivable that it could, on the basis of this Department's replies, permit deportation to any place at which the alien might again be taken into British custody. (National Archives of Ireland, DFA 369/8, 'Escaped Prisoners of War – Immunity from Deportation Back to Capture', memo by Rynne, 20 July 1948)

In other words, even if the court turned down the prisoner's plea against his expulsion, because External Affairs would have to admit that it had applied the 1907 and 1929 Conventions to belligerent service personnel in Ireland, the escaper could not be sent back to his original captor, which is precisely what de Valera ordered when German prisoners of war were transported back over the border into Northern Ireland.

Conclusion

The question of escape – both out of and into Eire – was one of the strangest and most difficult conundrums faced by the de Valera government during the war, and Dublin's attempt to tackle it further highlighted the contradictions inherent in its attitude towards belligerent internment. The men in the Curragh, officially classified as military internees from 1942 onwards, came under the protection of the 1929 Convention, meaning that their escape attempts were punished at the minimum standard handed out to prisoners of war. In practice, the Irish military usually suspended parole for a short period and their escape attempts were never met with deadly force. Germans attempting to reach Eire from camps in Northern Ireland were unilaterally categorised by the government as aliens, despite genuinely being prisoners of war, in order to *prevent* the 1907 convention being applied to them, meaning that Dublin could avoid having to allow them enter the country and taking responsibility for them once they arrived. This broke with other neutral practices in Europe. Switzerland assisted escaping prisoners of war to reach their own forces; although Spain arrested members of the belligerent forces who crossed its borders, Madrid held them only to ascertain their identities and then released them to the relevant diplomatic representatives.

In dealing with both military internees in Ireland and escaping German prisoners of war, the government prioritised its relationship

DOI: 10.1057/9781137446039.0007

with the Allies over its responsibilities as a neutral. The decision to avoid injuring or killing internees by not firing during escapes and the extremely lenient penalties for attempted breakout – in direct contrast to Switzerland – were motivated by a desire to steer clear of any complications with the Allied governments. As has already been proved, consular officials regularly visited K-Lines and any mistreatment or injury could very quickly lead to a major diplomatic confrontation. This leniency over escape fits in with the overall attitude of the government to allow the internees the maximum latitude possible, although the Department of Defence was very much of the opinion that this severely restricted the military's ability to contain the internees. Colonel McNally and his staff saw their task in simple terms: to guard the internees and prevent them from escaping the camp, and the use of live ammunition was a logical extension of this. However, External Affairs had a much broader view of the situation, having to integrate Ireland's relationship with the belligerents into its duties as a neutral. Invariably, when these two clashed, de Valera almost always opted to preserve Ireland's relationship with the Allies, no doubt calculating that neutrality would be easier to maintain if good relations were preserved with the warring nations.

Notes

1   Irish Military Archives, PM633, letter from Cowper to McNally, 20 July 1941.
2   Irish Military Archives, S/231, McNally to Adjutant-General, 4 September 1940.
3   Irish Military Archives, 3/42633, 'Members of the Belligerent Armed Forces interned at the Curragh Camp', December 1940.
4   National Archives of Ireland, DFA 241/309, Ua Moráin to Walshe, 27 June 1944.
5   National Archives of Ireland, DFA A/44, 'Duties of Military Policemen on Patrol Duty', 16 January 1941.
6   National Archives of Ireland, DFA A/44, 'Special Orders for Guard Commander', 21 March 1941.
7   Irish Military Archives, PM 1426, 'Special Orders for Sentinels', no date.
8   National Archives of Ireland, TAOIS S12212, 'Extract from Standing Orders for No.1 internment camp'.
9   National Archives of Ireland, TAOIS S11925/A, text of Emergency Powers Order no.28.
10 Irish Military Archives, A229A, McNally to Quartermaster General, 28 January 1941.
11 National Archives of Ireland, DFA A/44, 'Draft Aide-Mémoir', no date.

DOI: 10.1057/9781137446039.0007

12   Irish Military Archives, 3/42633, 'British Internees', McNally to Adjutant-General, 4 July 1941.

13   National Archives of Ireland, DFA A/44, 'Escape of British Internees', 26 June 1941.

14   National Archives of Ireland, DFA A/44, 'Attempted escape of Interned Members of the British and Allied Air Forces from B. Internment Camp, Curragh Camp on the 9th February 1942.'

15   National Archives of Ireland, DFA A/44, 'Special Orders for Guard Commander', 21 March 1941.

16   Irish Military Archives, PM 712, findings of Court of Enquiry, 16 July 1941.

17   National Archives of Ireland, DFA A/44, aide – mémoire from Hempel, 25 July 1941.

18   National Archives of Ireland, DFA A/44, 're Escapes of British Internees – Questions of "Parole" and "Restitution"', memo by Rynne, 30 July 1941.

19   National Archives of Ireland, DFA A/44, McNally to Adjutant-General, 8 January 1942.

20   National Archives of Ireland, DFA A/44, McMahon to Walshe, 24 January 1942.

21   National Archives of Ireland, DFA A/44, statement by Maffey, 16 February 1942.

22   National Archives of Ireland, DFA A/44, memo by Rynne, 10 February 1942.

23   National Archives of Ireland, DFA A/44, note by Boland, 22 January 1942.

24   Irish Military Archives, PM 335/1, Guiney to Provost Marshal, 18 October 1944.

25   National Archives of Ireland, DFA 241/342, Boland to Hankinson, 15 December 1942.

26   National Archives of Ireland, DFA A/26, 'Summary of chronological list of forced landings, or crashes of belligerent aircraft from the outbreak of war to 30.6.45', undated list.

27   Irish Military Archives, 3/42633, Walshe to Defence, 5 July 1941.

28   Tanner, *Refuge from the Reich*, p. 195.

29   Meares, 'Better off as Prisoners of War', 186.

30   Meares, 'Better off as Prisoners of War', 190.

31   National Archives of Ireland, DFA A/44, 're Action to be taken against British Internees', 11 February 1942.

32   Irish Military Archives, PM 712, Court of Enquiry findings, 16 July 1941.

33   Irish Military Archives, 3/42633, Walshe to MacMahon, 5 July 1941.

34   Dwyer, *Behind the Green Curtain*, p. 204.

35   Dwyer, *Behind the Green Curtain*, p. 204.

36   Irish Military Archives, PM 1426, Ringrose to O/C Eastern Command, 4 February 1944.

37   Irish Military Archvies, PM 1426, undated sketch diagram of No.4 camp.

DOI: 10.1057/9781137446039.0007

38   Public Record Office of Northern Ireland, HA 32/1/887, Younger to
     Gransden, 21 December 1944.
39   Public Record Office of Northern Ireland, HA 32/1/887, Kelly to Gransden,
     2 January 1945.
40   Public Record Office of Northern Ireland, HA 32/1/887, Warnock to Maynard
     Sinclair, 22 December 1944.
41   Public Record Office of Northern Ireland, CAB 9/CD/254/1, draft letter to
     Morrison, 20 October 1944.
42   National Archives of Ireland, DFA A/67, memo by Walshe, 16 January 1945.
43   B. Moore (1997) 'Turning Liabilities into Assets: British Government Policy
     towards German and Italian Prisoners of War during the Second World War',
     Journal of Contemporary History, 32, 1, 131.
44   See B. Moore (2006) 'Uninvited Guests in Troubled Times: German
     Prisoners of War in the Union of South Africa, 1942–1943' *The Journal of
     Military History*, 70, 1, 63–90.
45   Public Record Office of Northern Ireland, HA 32/1/887, Kelly to Grandsen,
     2 January 1945.
46   Public Record Office of Northern Ireland, HA 32/1/887, Younger to
     Grandsen, 21 December 1944.
47   Public Record Office of Northern Ireland, HA 32/1/887, Kelly to Gilfillan,
     9 January 1945.
48   A. Jackson (2010) *Churchill's Unexpected Guests: Prisoners of War in Britain in
     World War II.* (Gloucestershire: The History Press).
49   *Belfast News Letter*, 'German Prisoners in Ulster', 4 January 1945.
50   *Daily Mail* (Irish edition), 'Spate of Nazis for N. Ireland', 19 December 1944.
51   Public Record Office of Northern Ireland, HA 32/1/887, Kenney to Maynard
     Sinclair, 30 December 1944. 'Free Stater' was a derogatory term referring to
     Eire.
52   Fisk, *In Time of War*, p. 378.
53   International Committee of the Red Cross, https://www.icrc.org/applic/ihl/
     ihl.nsf/Article.xsp?action=openDocument&documentId=9490383D7B8FA4
     BDC12563CD00516A3B [Accessed 28 November 2014].
54   National Archives of Ireland, DFA A/67, 'Re: Escaped Prisoners of War in
     Neutral Territory', 12 December 1944.
55   National Archives of Ireland, DFA A/67 'Escaped Prisoners of War in Neutral
     Territory', 5 January 1945.
56   National Archives of Ireland, DFA A/67, 'Prisoners of War in the Six
     Counties', memo by Walshe 16 January 1945.
57   National Archives of Ireland, DFA A/67 'Escaped Prisoners of War in Neutral
     Territory', 5 January 1945.
58   National Archives of Ireland, DFA A/67, 'Prisoners of War in the Six
     Counties', memo by Walshe 16 January 1945.

DOI: 10.1057/9781137446039.0007

59   National Archives of Ireland, DFA A/67, 'Prisoners of War in the Six Counties', memo by Walshe 16 January 1945.
60   Irish Military Archives, PM 1701, Bryan to Provost Marshal, 12 January 1945.
61   Irish Military Archives, PM 1701, Bryan to Provost Marshal, 12 January 1945.
62   National Archives of Ireland, DFA A/67, Rynne to Walshe, 13 January 1945.
63   National Archives of Ireland, DFA A/67, McDonagh to Commissioner, 18 January 1945.
64   Irish Statute Book, http://www.irishstatutebook.ie/1935/en/act/pub/0014/sec0005.html#sec5 [Accessed 28 November 2014].
65   National Archives of Ireland, DFA 369/5, 'Re: The Germans at Cork', 21 January 1945.
66   National Archives of Ireland, DFA A/67, 'Prisoners of War in the Six Counties', memo by Walshe 16 January 1945.
67   National Archives of Ireland, DFA A/67, 'Prisoners of War in the Six Counties', memo by Walshe 16 January 1945.
68   National Archives of Ireland, DFA A/67, 'Control of Aliens coming from Northern Ireland', 16 January 1945.
69   National Archives of Ireland, DFA A/67, 'Stopped by censor I. Independent', 17 January 1945.
70   *Daily Express*, 'Ulster Germans Escape', 17 January 1945.
71   National Archives of Ireland, DFA A/67, Bryan to Walshe, 10 July 1945.
72   National Archives of Ireland, DFA A/67, interrogation report by British police, undated.
73   National Archives of Ireland, DFA A/67, note by Walshe, 10 July 1945.
74   National Archives of Ireland, DFA A/67, 'Prisoners of War in the Six Counties', memo by Walshe 16 January 1945.
75   National Archives of Ireland, DFA A/67, 'Control of aliens coming from Northern Ireland', 16 January 1945.
76   Irish Military Archives, PM 1701, Bryan to Provost Marshal, 12 January 1945.
77   National Archives of Ireland, DFA A/67, McDonagh to Commissioner, 18 January 1945.
78   *Sunday Pictorial*, 'I.R.A. planning mass escape of 2000 Germans', 14 January 1945.
79   M. Sullivan (1979) *Thresholds of Peace: Four Hundred Thousand German Prisoners and the People of Britain* (London: Hamish Hamilton), p. 97.
80   Public Record Office of Northern Ireland, HA 32/1/887, Good to Home Affairs, 1 August 1945.
81   Public Record Office of Northern Ireland, HA 32/1/887, Good to Home Affairs, 5 December 1945.
82   National Archives of Ireland, DFA 369/5, Connolly to External Affairs, 25 January 1946.
83   *Irish Times*, 'Kinsale War Victims Resent German Seamen', 23 January 1946.

DOI: 10.1057/9781137446039.0007

84 *Irish Times*, 'German Prisoners Doff Uniforms at Kinsale', 22 January 1946.

85 National Archives of Ireland, DFA 369/5, 'Re: the Germans at Kinsale', memo by Rynne, 21 January 1946.

86 National Archives of Ireland, DFA 369/5, O'Neill to Walshe, 1 March 1946.

87 National Archives of Ireland, DFA 369/5, Walshe to O'Neill, 19 March 1946.

88 National Archives of Ireland, DFA 369/5, Parliamentary question, 7 March 1946.

89 National Archives of Ireland, DFA 369/5, 'Extract from Official Report British House of Commons Debate 8 March, 1946'.

90 R. Winder (2013) *Bloody Foreigners: The Story of Immigration to Britain* (London: Abacus), p. 323.

91 National Archives of Ireland, DFA 369/5, 'Note for the Minister's information', 25 June 1946.

92 National Archives of Ireland, DFA 369/5, 're Deputy O'Neill's question' note for de Valera by Rynne, 6 March 1946.

93 National Archives of Ireland, DFA 369/5, Boland to Costigan, 7 February 1946.

DOI: 10.1057/9781137446039.0007

Conclusion: 'Not Breaking but Making International Law'?

Kelly, Bernard. *Military Internees, Prisoners of War and the Irish State during the Second World War.* Basingstoke: Palgrave Macmillan, 2015. DOI: 10.1057/9781137446039.0008.

▶

On 13 August 1945, 254 of the German internees left the Curragh and boarded a British warship docked in Dublin port to return to their homes.[1] Having been given a 48-hour parole to tie up their personal affairs in Ireland, 12 of the internees did not report back and went on the run from the Irish authorities. The descriptions and known associates list circulated to the Gardaí searching for these men shows just how close they and civilians who corresponded with them were watched by both the police and G2, and the names of those whom the internees were 'friendly with' were listed along with their addresses. The Gardaí were instructed that the power to arrest them derived from Emergency Powers Order no.170, the emergency legislation created to intern the men in the first place.[2] Four of these were eventually granted leave to remain in Ireland,[3] the other eight were recaptured and handed over to the British forces in Northern Ireland, the last being transferred in April 1946.[4] Remarkably, two of the men were reportedly caught in the grounds of the house of Mark Killilea, TD for Galway East;[5] when no action was taken against Killilea, the government came under pressure in the Dáil from independent TD James Dillon. After being pressed by Dillon, Minister for Justice Gerald Boland admitted that he was not 'saying it is a proper course of conduct' to hide fugitives from the police, but said that, in his opinion, there was no need to pursue a prosecution.[6] Shortly after the Germans had left, Oliver Flanagan asked de Valera if they had been sent home at the request of the British government. The Taoiseach, no doubt glad to be rid of them, even only if it meant that Flanagan would cease questioning the government about its internment policy, replied that they had been repatriated 'In accordance with international practice' but that 'Arrangements had to be made with the British authorities for their transport, and for their entry into Germany'.[7] In a way, this represented the internment policy as a whole: outwardly modelled on international precedents, but actually dependant on the Allies in its implementation.

The Irish belligerent internment policy during the Second World War needs to be viewed within the broader context of Irish concessions towards the Allies. Because it was anchored within neutrality – it would not have existed if Eire had not been neutral – the internment regime was heavily geared towards cooperating with the Allies, as neutrality was as a whole. It is well known that the de Valera government was willing to cooperate in minor matters with the Allies, while refusing to grant more public concessions such as the use of Irish ports or the expulsion of Axis representatives. Repeated landings and incursions by

DOI: 10.1057/9781137446039.0008

British aircraft in the early days of the war were ignored and it was not until August 1940 that the government – reluctantly – detained the first belligerent airmen. Even when Dublin was forced into a more balanced stance during 1940–41, some British pilots were interned but many more British aircraft, fliers and sailors were still released after making landfall in Eire. The entry of the United States into the war moved Ireland even closer to the Allies and started the process whereby Dublin's internment system eventually shifted to one which operated solely against Germany. No document has yet been found which suggests the decision to release all American aircraft came about because of representations or pressure from Washington; it appears to have been a purely Irish decision, made to pre-empt any adverse reaction from America. The distinction between 'operational' and 'non-operational' flights which allowed this to happen was a cover for a policy which was already in operation, as it was only agreed between Joseph Walshe and David Gray in late 1942. US aircraft had been landing in Ireland since July and none had been detained by the time of the Walshe – Gray discussions. As Dwight Meares has found, all European neutrals found ways to tailor their internment regimes to favour the Allies as the war went on, and Ireland was no exception.[8]

The figures speak for themselves. According to the government's own calculations, 39 American aircraft and 275 American aircrew landed or crashed in Ireland and all were released. There is evidence that nine US sailors were rescued and returned by Irish ships. No further details about this have been unearthed in the archives, but it provides an interesting contrast to the fate of the German sailors rescued by the *Kerlogue*. One hundred and three British aircraft and 453 aircrew landed in Irish territory or Irish waters; of this total 159 were killed, 31 were interned, along with a few from Canada, New Zealand, Poland and France, and the rest were promptly returned. By way of contrast, 16 German aircraft and 80 aircrew landed in Ireland; of these, 54 were interned for the duration of the war and a further 24 were killed during their initial crashes.[9] One was recaptured after escape and was handed over the British; another was permitted to return to Germany having spent over two years in Irish hospitals, after he was critically injured when his aircraft crashed.[10] The internment of the 164 sailors in January 1944 and the crew of U-260 only added further weight to the pro-Allied bias inherent in the system. Presented with figures like these, it is hard to disagree with Robert Fisk when he describes Irish 'collusion' with the Allies regarding belligerent internment.[11]

DOI: 10.1057/9781137446039.0008

Dublin could, and did, claim that there was room within international regulations to justify the release of Allied pilots, or that Ireland was simply following European precedent. The lack of precise rules concerning internment and the fact that they were drafted largely before aircraft became a major factor in warfare meant that neutral countries could interpret them as they required or as their individual circumstances dictated. There was even a reasonable argument to suggest that Ireland was allowed to intern the German sailors in 1944. De Valera was happy to respect international law when it worked in Ireland's favour: when pressed by the Department of Defence to staunch the flow of Irish men and women joining the British forces in mid-1941, the cabinet took no action, noting that according to the International Convention Concerning the Rights and Duties of Neutral Powers and Persons in War on Land, a neutral would not be held responsible if its citizens 'cross the frontier individually to offer their services to one of the belligerents'.[12] However, in two respects Dublin departed from neutral practice and in so doing undermined its own claims to being a genuinely neutral country during the war. While the release of the bulk of the Allied pilots in October 1943 could be defended as a retrospective application of the non-operational rule, the release of the remaining 11 in June 1944 cannot, and was based entirely on a need to maintain a cordial relationship with the Allies. There was no suggestion of an equal number of Germans being released in 1944, nor any attempt to categorise it as a neutral act. As the External Affairs note said, it was designed as 'a friendly gesture' towards the Allies, with no regard for balance or international law. It marked the final stage in the evolution of the Irish internment policy towards an undisguised pro-Allied stance.

The second was the decision to deny German prisoners of war entry to Eire when escaping from Northern Ireland. While the right of the Dublin government to regulate immigration and control the illegal entry of foreigners is undisputed, the decision on German escapers can still be characterised as an action at odds with neutrality. Faced with a set of unpalatable scenarios regarding escaping German prisoners, the de Valera government simply changed the rules before the game had ended. Classifying escapers as aliens rather than prisoners of war and using peacetime legislation to exclude them from Irish territory was a calculated attempt to avoid Ireland's duties as a neutral. Providing refuge for escaping prisoners of war might have prompted more to seek sanctuary in Eire, and any large body of German personnel loose in Ireland

DOI: 10.1057/9781137446039.0008

would have had considerable international repercussions for Dublin. De Valera had already incurred the wrath of the Allied governments and public for not expelling Axis diplomats in February 1944, and acting as a safe harbour for escaping German prisoners would undoubtedly have further tarnished Ireland's international reputation. In this, as is so many aspects of the belligerent internment policy, diplomatic considerations were the overriding priority.

But this justification, rational though it is, should not allow the de Valera government to escape criticism. Although Dublin kept its hands clean by not returning the few escapers directly to the British authorities, shoving them across the border into Northern Ireland, where they would almost certainly be recaptured, was tantamount to returning them to their captor – a decidedly unneutral act. The secrecy in which Dublin cloaked this decision, keeping it out of the media as well as the Dáil and thus shielding it from both public and political scrutiny, shows that de Valera knew that he was on dangerous ground. He was fortunate in 1945 that he was leading a Fianna Fáil government with an overall majority and did not have to explain his decisions to political partners; by way of contrast, the Swedish wartime coalition threatened to break up over German demands to send troops across Swedish territory in 1941.[13] It is decisions and acts such those concerning Allied pilots and German prisoners of war that lend credence to Trevor Salmon's argument that the Irish position during the war was not one of neutrality, but can best be described as non-belligerency.[14]

The bias clearly visible at the top level of internment was not replicated on the ground in K-Lines and subsequent belligerent camps in Ireland. The treatment offered to each group of internees was scrupulously fair, which is in contrast to the situation within Spain: for instance, different nationalities were given varying treatment within the Miranda de Ebro camp.[15] On the whole, however, conditions within the Irish belligerent camps were much the same as in others across neutral Europe, and the archival evidence shows that External Affairs consistently looked abroad for guidelines when framing policy on day-to-day issues. Accounts from Switzerland shows that military internees were offered parole, were loosely confined, allowed to interact with civilians and were provided with employment if they desired. The one significant difference was that the Swiss did not apply the 1929 convention to belligerent airmen, meaning that the penalty for attempted escape in Switzerland was far harsher than in Ireland. But, for the most part,

DOI: 10.1057/9781137446039.0008

belligerent internment in Ireland was very similar to other European neutrals. Life in the Curragh, even though it could be boring, cold and uncomfortable, was nothing like the life of a prisoner of war and should not be compared to one.

When dealing with prisoners of war held abroad, Irish or otherwise, Dublin adopted the appropriate attitude. External Affairs argued – correctly – that Ireland could not be responsible for the welfare or representation of Irish citizens who had freely chosen to join the forces of a belligerent, and insisted throughout the war that Ireland could not support Irish personnel captured by the Axis. Despite sporadic efforts to intervene on behalf of individual prisoners, Dublin was hampered by the fact that it had no legal standing to assist Irish prisoners and the Irish diplomatic network was very small at the time. When veterans, former prisoners of war amongst them, returned to Ireland after 1945, the government did not offer them any special concessions or facilities. Instead, it cooperated closely with the British government to ensure that all veterans received the benefits of their service from Britain. For instance, de Valera sanctioned special medical boards in Dublin and Cork, consisting of two local doctors, a British Ministry of Pensions doctor and a Finance Officer from Northern Ireland, to assess the health of returned Irish prisoners and to determine what benefits would be paid to them.[16] In addition, if they required medical aid, they would be cared for in Irish hospitals, paid for by the British government, or offered hospital places in Northern Ireland.

The main area in which Dublin was extremely lax was in its attitude towards the sending of prisoner parcels from Ireland. It should have been obvious to the government that some form of mail service to prisoners of war abroad was required, given the large number of Irish in the British forces even before the war broke out. The fact that it took until 1943 to sanction a free parcel scheme is a reflection of the sluggish-ness with which the government moved. Boland was correct when he acknowledged – belatedly – that Eire had a moral duty to provide such a scheme, even if the government had not ratified the 1929 convention. The delay caused unnecessary distress to many Irish families who also had to bear the cost of sending next-of-kin packages for the majority of the war.

In conclusion, the de Valera government during the Second World War followed a convoluted strategy of partially implementing, partly ignoring and sometimes bypassing international law and regulations

DOI: 10.1057/9781137446039.0008

regarding military internees and prisoners of war. In some aspects, Ireland was a model neutral; in others, *realpolitik* dictated the jettisoning of whole sections of international convention. A policy of precise and textbook neutrality was incompatible with de Valera's public promise in 1935 not to allow Irish territory to be used to attack Britain; therefore the government consistently prioritised the relationship with the Allies when the two issues clashed. Michael Rynne consoled himself and Joseph Walshe that Ireland was 'not breaking but making international law'[17] by adopting an extremely flexible attitude towards belligerent internment, but it that was a long way from the 'strict neutrality' that the Irish minister in the Vatican was reminded to project in June 1941. De Valera's inconsistent approach to neutrality during the Second World War was the beginning of many years of governmental ambiguity towards what actually constituted Irish neutrality and how it applied to the post-war world.

Notes

1 The National Archives, CAB 129/2, 'Report for the month of August 1945 for the Dominions, India, Burma, and the Colonies and Mandated Territories', 2 October 1945.
2 National Archives of Ireland, JUS 8/933 'German Internees who have broken parole', 13 September 1945.
3 Leach, *Fugitive Ireland*, p. 71.
4 Dwyer, *Behind the Green Curtain*, p. 335.
5 *Irish Independent*, 'Six German Internees now recaptured', 28 September 1945.
6 Dáil debates, 6 December 1945.
7 Dáil debates, 18 October 1945.
8 Meares, 'Neutral States and the Application of International Law', p. 101.
9 National Archives of Ireland, DFA A/26, 'Summary of chronological list of forced landings, or crashes of belligerent aircraft from the outbreak of war to the 30.6.45', undated list.
10 Irish Military Archives, PM 633/733, 'History of Eire's belligerent camps', no date.
11 Fisk, *In Time of War*, p. 176.
12 National Archives of Ireland, TAOIS S/6091A, 'Assistance being offered to Irish citizens to enlist in the British Army', 7 May 1941.
13 Scott, 'Swedish Midsummer crisis of 1941', 381.

DOI: 10.1057/9781137446039.0008

14   T.C. Salmon (1989) *Unneutral Ireland: An Ambivalent and Unique Security Policy* (Oxford: Clarendon Press), p. 118.

15   Eiroa, 'Uncertain Fates', 47.

16   National Archives of Ireland, DFA 341/11, unsigned memo, 5 May 1945.

17   National Archives of Ireland, DFA A/26, 'Theory and Practice relative to Belligerent Aircraft and Crews', Rynne to Walshe 30 October 1942.

DOI: 10.1057/9781137446039.0008

References

Archives

National Archives of Ireland

Department of Foreign Affairs (DFA)
Department of the Taoiseach (TAOIS)
Department of Justice (JUS)
Office of the Attorney-General (AGO)
Office of the Secretary of the President (PRES)

Irish Military Archives

Internment Subject Files

University College Dublin Archives

Bryan Papers (P71)
De Valera Papers (P150)

Columban Archives

Korea Papers (KOR)
Philippines Papers (PI)
Burma Papers (B)

Newspapers

Belfast Newsletter
Cork Examiner
Daily Express

DOI: 10.1057/9781137446039.0009

Daily Mail
Daily Telegraph
Irish Independent
The Kerryman
Irish News
Irish Press
Irish Times
Manchester Guardian
News Chronicle
Sunday Pictorial
Toronto Star

Magazines

History Ireland

Articles

J. Custodis (2011) 'Exploiting the Enemy in the Orkneys: The Employment of Italian Prisoner of War on the Scapa Flow Barriers during the Second World War' *Journal of Scottish Historical Studies*, 31, 1, 72–98.

M. Eiroa and C. Pallarés (2014) 'Uncertain Fates: Allied Soldiers at the Miranda de Ebro Concentration Camp' *The Historian*, 76, 1, 26–49.

K. Fedorowich and B. Moore (1996) 'Co-Belligerency and Prisoners of War: Britain and Italy, 1943–45' *The International History Review*, 18, 1, 28–47.

G.M. Hagglof (1960) 'A Test of Neutrality: Sweden in the Second World War' *International Affairs*, 36, 153–67.

J.A. Hellen (1999) 'Temporary Settlement and Transient Populations the Legacy of Britain's Prisoner of War camps: 1940–1948' *Erdkunde*, 53, 3, 191–219.

B. Kelly (2012) 'British Military Deserters in the Irish Free State, 1922–1932' *Studia Hibernica*, 38, 201–16.

O.J. Lizzityn (1953) 'The Treatment of Aerial Intruders in Recent Practice and International Law' *The American Journal of International Law*, 47, 4, 559–89.

S.P. MacKenzie (1994) 'The Treatment of Prisoners of War in World War II' *The Journal of Modern History*, 66, 3, 487–520.

DOI: 10.1057/9781137446039.0009

D.S. Meares (2013a) 'Better off as Prisoners of War. The Differential Standard of Protection for Military Internees in Switzerland during World War II' *Journal of the History of International Law*, 15, 173–99.

D.S. Meares (2013b) 'Neutral States and the Application of International Law to United States airmen during World War II. To Intern or Not to Intern?' *Journal of the History of International Law*, 15, 77–101.

B. Moore (1997) 'Turning Liabilities into Assets: British Government Policy towards German and Italian Prisoners of War during the Second World War' *Journal of Contemporary History*, 32, 1, 117–36.

B. Moore (2006) 'Unwanted Guests in Troubled Times: German Prisoners of War in the Union of South Africa, 1942–43' *Journal of Military History*, 70, 1, 63–90.

J.D. Morrow (2001) 'The Institutional Features of Prisoner of War Treaties' *International Organisation*, 55, 4, 971–91.

J.L. Rosenberg (1980) 'The 1941 Mission of Frank Aiken to the United States: An American Perspective' *Irish Historical Studies*, 22, 86, 162–77.

J. Reynolds (2008) 'It's a Long Way to Tipperary: German POWs in Templemore' *History Ireland*, 16, 3, 23–25.

C.G. Scott (2002) 'The Swedish Midsummer Crisis of 1941: The Crisis That Never War' *Journal of Contemporary History*, 37, 3, 371–94.

D.F. Vagts (1997) 'Switzerland, International Law and World War II' *The American Journal of International Law*, 91, 3, 466–75.

Books

A.J. Barker (1974) *Behind Barbed Wire* (London: BT Batsford Ltd).

T. Bartlett and K. Jeffery (1997) *A Military History of Ireland* (Cambridge: Cambridge University Press).

H. Boog, J. Förster, J. Hoffman, E. Klink, R.D. Müller and G.R. Ueberschär (eds.) (1996) *Germany and the Second World War Volume IV: The Attack on the Soviet Union* (Oxford: Clarendon Press).

P. Browne (2003) *Eagles over Ireland* (Athenry: Flying Fortress Athenry 1943 Project).

J. Clive (1983) *Broken Wings* (London: Granada).

T.P. Coogan (1993) *De Valera: Long Fellow, Long Shadow* (London: Hutchinson).

C. Crowe, et al. (2006) *Documents on Irish Foreign Policy Volume V: 1937–1939* (Dublin: Royal Irish Academy).

DOI: 10.1057/9781137446039.0009

C. Crowe, et al. (2008) *Documents on Irish Foreign Policy Volume VI: 1939–1941* (Dublin: Royal Irish Academy).

C. Crowe, et al. (2010) *Documents on Irish Foreign Policy Volume VII: 1941–1945* (Dublin: Royal Irish Academy).

R.M. Douglas (2009) *Architects of the Resurrection: Altirí na hAiséirrghe and the Fascist 'New Order' in Ireland* (Manchester: Manchester University Press).

T.R. Dwyer (1994) *Guests of the State: The Story of Allied and Axis Servicemen Interned in Ireland during World War II* (Dingle: Brandon).

T.R. Dwyer (2010) *Behind the Green Curtain: Ireland's Phoney Neutrality during World War II* (Dublin: Gill & Macmillan).

N. Ferguson (1998) *The Pity of War* (London: Penguin Books).

D. Ferriter (2005) *The Transformation of Ireland, 1900–2000* (London: Profile Books).

D. Ferriter (2007) *Judging Dev: A Reassessment of the Life and Legacy of Eamon de Valera* (Dublin: Royal Irish Academy).

R. Fisk (1985) *In Time of War: Ireland, Ulster and the Price of Neutrality, 1939–45* (Dublin: Gill & Macmillan).

B. Flynn (2011) *Pawns in the Game: Irish Hunger Strikes 1912–1981* (Cork: Collins Press).

D. Fraser (1983) *And We Shall Shock Them: The British Army in the Second World War* (London: Book Club Associates).

M. Gillies (2011) *The Barbed-Wire University: The Real Lives of Prisoners of War in the Second World War* (London: Aurum).

J. Gilmour (2010) *Sweden, the Swastika and Stalin: The Swedish Experience in the Second World War* (Edinburgh: Edinburgh University Press).

B. Girvin (2006) *The Emergency: Neutral Ireland, 1939–1945* (London: Plagrave Macmillan).

B. Girvin and G. Roberts (2000) *Ireland and the Second World War: Politics, Society and Remembrance* (Dublin: Four Courts Press).

B. Grob-Fitzgibbon (2004) *The Irish Experience during the Second World War: An Oral History* (Dublin: Irish Academic Press).

J. Harte and S. Meara (2007) *To the Limits of Endurance: One Irishman's War.* Dublin: Liberties Press.

M. Hastings (2004) *Armageddon: The Battle for Germany, 1944–45* (London: Palgrave Macmillan).

M. Hastings (2007) *Nemesis: The Battle for Japan, 1944–45* (London: Harper Perennial).

DOI: 10.1057/9781137446039.0009

W.I. Hitchcock (2009) *Liberation: The Bitter Road to Freedom, Europe 1944–1945* (London: Faber and Faber).

S. Jackson (2010) *Churchill's Unexpected Guests: Prisoners of War in Britain in World War II* (Gloucestershire: The History Press).

R. Keefer (2002) *Grounded in Eire: The Story of Two RAF Fliers Interned in Ireland during World War II* (Montreal: McGill-Queen's University Press).

B. Kelly (2012) *Returning Home: Irish Ex-servicemen after the Second World War* (Dublin: Merrion).

M. Kennedy (2008) *Guarding Neutral Ireland: The Coast Watching Service and Military Intelligence, 1939–1945* (Dublin: Four Courts Press).

M. Kennedy and V. Lang (2011) *The Irish Defence Forces 1940–1949: The Chiefs of Staff's Reports* (Dublin: Irish Manuscript Commission).

D. Keogh (2005) *Twentieth-Century Ireland: Revolution and State Building* (Dublin: Gill and Macmillan).

D. Keogh and M. O'Driscoll (2004) *Ireland in World War II: Neutrality and Survival* (Cork: Mercier Press).

I. Kershaw (2000) *Hitler 1936–1945: Nemesis* (London: Allen Lane the Penguin Press).

D. Leach (2009) *Fugitive Ireland: European Minority Nationalists and Irish Political Asylum, 1937–2008* (Dublin: Four Courts Press).

B. MacArthur (2005) *Surviving the Sword: Prisoners of the Japanese in the Far East, 1942–45* (New York: Random House).

J. Maguire (2008) *IRA Internments and the Irish Government: Subversives and the State, 1939–1962* (Dublin: Irish Academic Press).

D. MacCarron (2003) *Landfall Ireland: The Story of Allied and German Aircraft Which Came down in Éire in World War Two* (Newtownards: Colourpoint Books).

M. Mazower (1998) *Dark Continent: Europe's Twentieth Century* (London: Penguin Books).

J. Nichol and T. Rennell (2003) *The Last Escape: The Untold Story of Allied Prisoners of War in Germany 1944–45* (London: Penguin).

J. O'Carroll and J.A. Murphy (1983) *De Valera and His Times* (Cork: Cork University Press).

E. O'Halpin (2000) *Defending Ireland: The Irish State and Its Enemies* (Oxford: Oxford University Press).

E. O'Halpin (2003) *MI5 and Ireland 1939–1945: The Official History* (Dublin: Irish Academic Press).

T. O'Reilly (2008) *Hitler's Irishmen* (Cork: Mercier Press).

R. Overy (2014) *The Bombing War: Europe 1939–1945* (London: Penguin).

H. Patterson (2007) *Ireland since 1939: The Persistence of Conflict* (London: Penguin Books).

D. Power (1994) *Long Way from Tipperary* (Clonmel: Glen Publications).

P. Preston (1994) *Franco* (New York: Basic Books).

L. Rees (2008) *Their Darkest Hour* (London: Ebury Press).

T.C. Salmon (1989) *Unneutral Ireland: An Ambivalent and Unique Security Policy* (Oxford: Clarendon Press).

S. Scheipers (2010) *Prisoners in War* (Oxford: Oxford University Press).

M.B. Sullivan (1979) *Thresholds of Peace: Four Hundred Thousand German Prisoners and the People of Britain* (London: Hamish Hamilton).

S. Tanner (2000) *Refuge from the Reich: American Airmen and Switzerland during World War II* (New York: Sarpedon).

M. Walsh (2010) *G2 In Defence of Ireland: Irish Military Intelligence 1918–45* (Cork: Collins Press).

R. Widders (2012) *The Emperor's Irish Slaves: Prisoners of the Japanese in the Second World War* (Dublin: The History Press Ireland).

R. Winder (2013) *Bloody Foreigners: The Story of Immigration to Britain* (London: Abacus).

I.S. Wood (2002) *Ireland during the Second World War* (London: Caxton Editions).

I.S. Wood (2012) *Britain, Ireland and the Second World War* (Edinburgh: Edinburgh University Press).

N. Wyllie (2002) *European Neutrals and Non-Belligerents during the Second World War* (Cambridge: Cambridge University Press).

N. Wyllie (2003) *Britain, Switzerland and the Second World War* (Oxford: Oxford University Press).

DOI: 10.1057/9781137446039.0009

Index

DOI: 10.1057/9781137446039.0010

DOI: 10.1057/9781137446039.0010

DOI: 10.1057/9781137446039.0010

Lightning Source UK Ltd.
Milton Keynes UK
UKOW04n2340110815

256754UK00002B/16/P